CliffsNotes™
Getting on the Internet

By David Crowder and Rhonda Crowder

IN THIS BOOK

- Choose an Internet service provider and send and receive e-mail

- Select a browser, set your home page, and visit sites anywhere on the World Wide Web

- Download free software, get expert advice, and keep up with the news

- Chat online and meet kindred spirits in Internet communities

- Reinforce what you learn with CliffsNotes Review

- Find more information about the Internet in CliffsNotes Resource Center and online at www.cliffsnotes.com

IDG Books Worldwide, Inc.
An International Data Group Company

Foster City, CA • Chicago, IL • Indianapolis, IN • New York, NY

IDG BOOKS
WORLDWIDE

About the Author

David and Rhonda Crowder were selling hypertext systems back when few people knew what the term *hypertext* meant. They have been involved in the online community for over a decade. Their Web site designs include the award-winning LinkFinder (www.linkfinder.com) and NetWelcome (www.netwelcome.com) sites, and they are the authors or coauthors of over a dozen books, including *Setting Up an Internet Site For Dummies* and the bestselling *Teach Yourself the Internet*.

Publisher's Acknowledgments

Editorial

Project Editors: Jeanne S. Criswell, Rev Mengle

Acquisitions Editor: Andy Cummings

Copy Editors: Constance Carlisle, Ted Cains

Technical Editor: Bill Karow

Editorial Assistant: Jamila Pree

Production

Indexer: York Production Services

Proofreader: York Production Services

IDG Books Indianapolis Production Department

CliffsNotes™ Getting on the Internet

Published by
IDG Books Worldwide, Inc.
An International Data Group Company
919 E. Hillsdale Blvd.
Suite 400
Foster City, CA 94404
www.idgbooks.com (IDG Books Worldwide Web site)
www.cliffsnotes.com (Cliffs Notes Web site)

Library of Congress Catalog Card No.: 99-64900

ISBN:0-7645-8526-6

Printed in the United States of America

10 9 8 7 6 5 4 3 2 1

1O/TR/QY/ZZ/IN

Distributed in the United States by IDG Books Worldwide, Inc.

Distributed by CDG Books Canada Inc. for Canada; by Transworld Publishers Limited in the United Kingdom; by IDG Norge Books for Norway; by IDG Sweden Books for Sweden; by IDG Books Australia Publishing Corporation Pty. Ltd. for Australia and New Zealand; by TransQuest Publishers Pte Ltd. for Singapore, Malaysia, Thailand, Indonesia, and Hong Kong; by Gotop Information Inc. for Taiwan; by ICG Muse, Inc. for Japan; by Norma Comunicaciones S.A. for Colombia; by Intersoft for South Africa; by Eyrolles for France; by International Thomson Publishing for Germany, Austria and Switzerland; by Distribuidora Cuspide for Argentina; by LR International for Brazil; by Ediciones ZETA S.C.R. Ltda. for Peru; by WS Computer Publishing Corporation, Inc., for the Philippines; by Contemporanea de Ediciones for Venezuela; by Express Computer Distributors for the Caribbean and West Indies; by Micronesia Media Distributor, Inc. for Micronesia; by Grupo Editorial Norma S.A. for Guatemala; by Chips Computadoras S.A. de C.V. for Mexico; by Editorial Norma de Panama S.A. for Panama; by American Bookshops for Finland. Authorized Sales Agent: Anthony Rudkin Associates for the Middle East and North Africa.

For general information on IDG Books Worldwide's books in the U.S., please call our Consumer Customer Service department at **800-762-2974**. For reseller information, including discounts and premium sales, please call our Reseller Customer Service department at **800-434-3422**.

For information on where to purchase IDG Books Worldwide's books outside the U.S., please contact our International Sales department at 317-596-5530 or fax **317-596-5692**.

For consumer information on foreign language translations, please contact our Customer Service department at **1-800-434-3422**, fax **317-596-5692**, or e-mail rights@idgbooks.com.

For information on licensing foreign or domestic rights, please phone +**1-650-655-3109**.

For sales inquiries and special prices for bulk quantities, please contact our Sales department at 650-655-3200 or write to the address above.

For information on using IDG Books Worldwide's books in the classroom or for ordering examination copies, please contact our Educational Sales department at **800-434-2086** or fax **317-596-5499**.

For press review copies, author interviews, or other publicity information, please contact our Public Relations department at **650-655-3000** or fax **650-655-3299**.

For authorization to photocopy items for corporate, personal, or educational use, please contact Copyright Clearance Center, 222 Rosewood Drive, Danvers, MA 01923, or fax **978-750-4470**.

Table of Contents

INTRODUCTION

While most of us were still getting used to the idea of computers, a revolution was underway in the way people use computers. Basically, the idea was that if one computer is good, two or more are better. If you link them together, each computer can have different software and data on it, but you can use any computer in the chain and take advantage of the full complement of resources on all of them. As a result, the *computer network* was born.

The next step was to connect two networks together. After this achievement, hooking together all the networks in the world was only a matter of time. This network of networks was called an *internetwork* and came to be known as the *Internet*. Today, the Internet is a major part of modern life for millions of people — surfing the World Wide Web, exchanging e-mail with friends and coworkers, and sharing interests with new acquaintances from around the world in live chat rooms.

Why Do You Need This Book?

Can you answer yes to any of these questions?

- Do you need to learn how to get on the Internet fast?
- Don't have time to read a 500-page book about the Internet?
- Do you need to know how e-mail works?
- Do you want to understand how to use online chat?
- Do you want to listen to live music from the Internet?

If so, then CliffsNotes *Getting on the Internet* is for you!

How to Use This Book

You're the boss here. You decide how to use this book. You can either read the book from cover to cover or just look for the information you want and then put the book back on the shelf for later. However, we recommend here a few ways to search for your topic(s).

■ Use the index in the back of the book to find what you're looking for.

■ Flip through the book looking for your topic in the running heads.

■ Look for your topic in the Table of Contents in the front of the book.

■ Look at the "In This Chapter" list at the beginning of each chapter.

■ Look for additional information in the CliffsNotes Resource Center or test your knowledge in the CliffsNotes Review.

■ Or flip through the book until you find what you're looking for — because we organized the book in a logical, task-oriented way.

Also, to find important information quickly, you can look for icons strategically placed in the text. Here is a description of the icons you find in this book:

If you see a Remember icon, make a mental note of this text — it's worth keeping in mind.

If you see a Tip icon, you know that you've run across a helpful hint, uncovered a secret, or received helpful advice.

If you see a Warning icon, you need to watch out for something that can be dangerous, requires special caution, or should be avoided.

Don't Miss Our Web Site

You may be new to the Internet, but this book helps you get online in no time flat. Make sure that our Web site at www.cliffsnotes.com is your first destination. Here's what you find there:

■ Interactive tools that are fun and informative

■ Links to interesting Web sites

■ Additional resources to help you continue your learning

At www.cliffsnotes.com, you can even register for a new feature called CliffsNotes Daily, which offers you newsletters on a variety of topics, delivered right to your e-mail inbox each business day.

See you at www.cliffsnotes.com!

CHAPTER 1
MAKING THE CONNECTION

IN THIS CHAPTER

- Understanding modems
- Picking a provider
- Managing your settings

If you're already connected to the Internet through work or at school, you can feel free to skip ahead to the other chapters. However, if you're connecting your personal computer from home, you need to take a look at a few basics.

This chapter focuses on modem connections because they're the single most common and least expensive method of connecting to the Internet. However, a number of ways to get hooked up to the Internet exist. They range from hooking up through your cable television provider to having specialized high-speed lines installed. The first option is currently beset with many problems because cable Internet connections are a fairly new and still developing technology, and the latter approach requires very deep pockets.

You also need an *Internet Service Provider* (ISP) to connect you to the Internet. This chapter shows you how to make that connection so that you're ready to become a *Netizen,* a citizen of the Internet.

Understanding Modems

Most people connect their personal computers to the Internet with a device called a *modem*. Modem is short for *modulator/dem*odulator; modulation and demodulation are technical terms for the manner in which the modem converts computer activity into signals that it can transmit and receive over telephone lines. Essentially, you can think of the modem as a telephone for your computer to use.

Modem speeds

Modems come in a variety of speeds. The speed of a modem refers to the amount of information that the modem can transmit or receive in a given amount of time, measured in *bits per second,* or *bps* for short. As modems have become faster and faster, the bps is now usually given in thousands of bits per second, or *kbps* (or just *k* for short), in order to avoid all the zeroes that now follow the speed rating. (Technically, the "K" means to multiply by 1,024, not 1,000, but it's close enough for horseshoes.) The higher the bps rating is, the faster you can upload or download files through that modem.

Here are the four modem speeds that you can probably find in your local computer store:

■   14.4K

■   28.8K

■   33.6K

■   56K

Generally, this is a case of "the faster, the better." The 56K speed (also called V.90) is today's standard, and most people use it. However, it may be exceeded by some other advance, and you may want to consider a few things before you plunk down big bucks for the latest advance in modem technology:

- If the fastest speed available has only recently come out, you may find that you're unable to get much use out of it. After all, the modem you use has to connect with another modem at your service provider. The ISP is probably using whatever is the currently accepted standard. If your modem is too new to be compatible with theirs, you're out of luck. At best, you can use the new modem in a scaled-back mode that may work with older modems.

- Slower modems are cheaper because they're less in demand. If your needs don't include being on the absolute leading edge, the slower modem is an option to consider. In fact, you may make some store manager's day by taking one off his hands; he may even be willing to drop the price if you ask.

Remember

Does this mean that you should avoid the hottest modems on the market? Not necessarily. Remember that modem speed advances always come with a catch — not only are new modems more expensive, but they invariably represent a new technology, which takes time to become a real standard. So you need to make sure that new modems have reached an acceptable level that guarantees

- Sales brisk enough to bring prices down to reasonable levels.

- A technology standard enough to be useful.

If these conditions exist, then you're much better off buying a faster modem. When you surf the Net, you really appreciate the advantages of speed.

Internal versus external modems

You can find two kinds of modems — internal and external. *Internal modems* look like other electronic cards that you insert into slots inside the case of your computer. If you've bought a computer in the last several years, then the odds are pretty good that an internal modem came as part of the computer's basic equipment.

External modems (see Figure 1-1) are small plastic or metal boxes that use a serial cable to connect to a serial port on the back of your computer. External modems require their own power supply, while internal modems draw their power from the computer itself.

Figure 1-1:   A typical external modem.

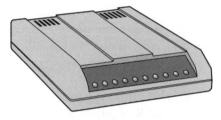

Each kind of modem has its advantages and disadvantages, as detailed in Table 1-1.

Table 1-1: Internal versus External Modems

Internal Modem Advantages	External Modem Advantages
✔ Less expensive	✔ Less complicated to hook up, so it's more easily moved from computer to computer
✔ Doesn't take up any desk space	✔ Can be turned on or off without having to reboot the computer
✔ Doesn't require additional electrical outlet	✔ Has indicator lights that keep you posted on all the gory goings-on so loved by techie types
✔ Won't add cable to the snaky mess behind the computer	

As the table shows, external modems are much easier to move from one computer to another. All you have to do is disconnect the serial cable from the computer the modem is hooked to and reconnect the cable to the new computer. You should disconnect the power supply and make sure that both the computer and the modem are turned off before doing this.

To move an internal modem, you have to go to quite a bit more trouble. Here's what to do:

1. Disconnect all power supplies.

2. Open up both computers.

3. Remove the phone cables from the modem.

4. Unscrew the internal modem card.

5. Pull the modem card from its slot and insert it into an available slot in the second computer.

6. Screw the modem card into place.

7. Put the covers back on both computers.

8. Reconnect the phone cables and then reconnect the power supplies.

9. Screw in a cover plate in the first computer to plug the hole you left in the back when you removed the internal modem.

Modem connection

Whether external or internal, the modem needs to connect to your telephone line using the same standard telephone cable that connects your home telephone to the phone jack in the wall. Modems almost always come with the telephone cable and/or other cables that you need. If yours doesn't or — as is often the case — the cable is too short to reach from your desk to the phone jack in the wall, you can pick up telephone cables in a variety of lengths at practically any store (even on the housewares aisle of a grocery store) for a reasonable cost. However, if you need a serial cable, you have to go to a computer or office supply store.

Typical modems use two separate telephone line connectors:

■ The connector that's usually labeled "line" hooks up to the telephone jack in your wall. Just plug one end of the telephone line into this connector and the other end into the wall jack. These days, everything with phone lines is done with modular plugs, and you only need to push the plug on the end of the phone line into the jack until you hear a click. If the plug doesn't go in easily, you may have it upside down; turn it over and try again.

■ The other connector is usually labeled "phone" (some labels show a drawing of a telephone). This connector is not actually necessary for using the modem; it's there in case you want to hook up a telephone, too. You just plug the phone cable from your telephone into this connector the same way you plug a phone into the wall jack. If your connectors aren't labeled (which is rare, but we've seen it happen), you need to consult the user manual for the modem to see which one is which. If you don't have a manual, just try each one.

Even if you don't plan to use a phone on the same line as your modem, hooking a phone up to the line is a good idea. That way, if things go wrong, you can tell if the problem's in the phone line. With the computer (or modem, if it's external) turned off, just pick up the phone and see if you hear a dial tone.

On an external modem, you normally find these connectors on the back of the box. With an internal modem, you can find these connectors on the part of the modem card that protrudes through the back of your computer.

The diagram in Figure 1-2 shows how a typical external modem is connected. For an internal modem, the connections are the same, except that you don't have to deal with the serial cable and power cord.

Figure 1-2:   Connecting the modem.

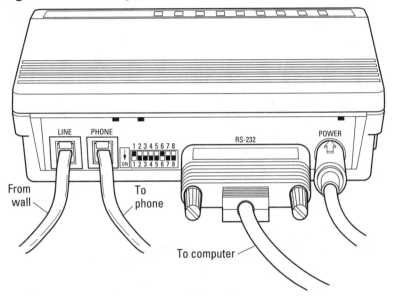

Most people plug the power supplies for both their computers and modems into a *surge suppressor,* which is a special kind of extension cord, usually with multiple outlets, that helps to eliminate possible damage from irregularities in electrical current. You also can find a similar gadget for eliminating power surges in the phone line itself. We highly recommend using both kinds of surge suppressors. If you use an *Uninterruptible Power Supply (UPS)* — a kind of battery keeps your system going during a brief power outage — you shouldn't need to purchase extra surge suppression. Most UPS systems have both power line surge suppression and phone line surge suppression built in.

Plugging a modem into a surge suppressor or UPS unit often reduces the throughput of the modem.

Always get offline and turn off your equipment during a lightning storm. You may even want to unplug everything as well. No matter what anyone tells you, no surge suppressor can stop a lightning strike from frying your equipment — and maybe you.

Picking an Internet Service Provider

After your hardware is all set up, you need to make a connection to an *Internet service provider* (or *ISP,* for short). An ISP provides you with a telephone number that you can set your modem to dial. After the modem at that number answers and connects with your modem, you're patched into the ISP's computer network and connected through it to the Internet.

Local versus national ISPs

All sorts of ISPs are available for you, ranging from little mom-n-pop setups to huge outfits, such as America Online (AOL) and Prodigy. Of course, not all local ISPs are small companies. True, some are nothing more than a few networked computers and some high-speed phone lines running out of a spare room, but many of them are first-class operations that can put major corporations to shame when it comes to performance and service. When considering whether to go local or national, keep some of these points in mind:

■ Although a local ISP may have more limited facilities, you may actually find connecting to the Internet through them easier because you have less competition for the limited number of phone lines available at any given time.

- Most national ISPs have extended hours for technical support, which can be a blessing when you have a problem in the wee hours. On the other hand, local ISPs tend to care more about keeping their customers and are often more helpful to you.

- If you travel, logging on to a local ISP back at your home base means making long-distance calls, which increases your expenditures for Internet access. A national ISP has local access phone numbers in all the major cities, meaning you can probably connect to them with a local call wherever you go.

- Some national ISPs, like AOL and Prodigy, were originally separate online services before they began to offer Internet access, and their main focus is still their proprietary content, which is meant to keep you within their own systems. If that content fulfills your needs, that's fine — you can still jump onto the Internet anytime. But if your main desire is to bypass such proprietary content and get out onto the Internet, you may want to choose an ISP that is solely dedicated to that purpose. Companies such as UUNet and EarthLink are. Ask them before you hand over your money.

- If you need to have some specialized equipment installed (such as for high-speed access), local ISPs are usually better geared toward making arrangements for delivery and installation than a company from outside the area. Some national ISPs don't even offer any alternatives to the normal connection arrangements. Others are specialists in the field; UUNet, for instance, is an old hand at providing Internet access at any level. (The odds are pretty good that your local ISP actually uses UUNet for their own access.)

All ISPs have more customers than they have phone lines. They gamble that only a small percentage of people will try to connect at the same time.

Prices for Internet access generally range from about $10 to $20 per month for unlimited usage. However, the term *unlimited* is usually not really true. Make sure that you read the fine print in your user agreement. You may have to get off when you're not actively using the Internet, and you probably get dumped automatically if you're not running some Internet program like a Web browser or e-mail at the time the ISP becomes overloaded. (AOL, in particular, is notorious for nagging its customers to get offline.) If you really need a full-time connection, you can actually stay on 24 hours a day without your ISP squawking if you pay them about $50 a month. Or if you can handle having to log off only once a day, you can try EarthLink, a major national ISP with tons of local access phone numbers, which lets you stay on all the time for $19.95 a month. Check out their Web site at www.earthlink.net or call them toll–free at 1-888-327-8454.

The vast majority of $10-per-month offers are nothing more than introductory rates that turn into $20-per-month fees after the first month or two.

Internet access fees will probably continue to drop rather than increase, and attempts to charge by the hour will continue to fail under the political pressure of the powerful Netizen voting bloc.

For something in between the local ISP and the national online service, check out UUNet, a major national ISP. They can be reached at 1-800-488-6384. Their Web site is at www.uunet.com.

How to locate an ISP

The major national online services such as America Online, CompuServe, and Prodigy are the easiest to find. They're in every major city, and their software is available in most bookstores and practically every computer store. Just pick up one of the free CD-ROMs lying around the checkout counter (just to be on the safe side, make sure that the clerks know the CD is free before you waltz out the door with it).

If you can't find a freebie trial CD in a store, you may find it as an attachment to a major computer magazine. And you probably get enough of them in the mail to build a small fortress if you're on computer-related mailing lists.

If none of these methods appeals to you, you can always give the national online services a call on their toll-free numbers:

- America Online: 1-800-827-6364

- CompuServe: 1-800-848-8199

- Prodigy: 1-800-213-0992

CompuServe is owned by America Online, but is still operated as an independent online service.

Back in 1997, all three major national online services ended up in trouble with the Federal Trade Commission regarding their "free membership" offers. Be aware that, if you do sign up for a free offer, you're automatically billed membership fees after the first month of the trial offer. Theoretically, this billing requires written permission on your part, but some of these national ISPs have occasionally overlooked that technical detail. In fairness, many local ISPs follow the same procedure. Buyer beware.

To find a local ISP, pay attention to ads on television or radio or in local newspapers. Also, you can usually find several ISPs by calling your local computer stores and asking for recommendations. And of course, don't neglect the Yellow Pages — check under Internet Services.

If you're already on the Internet, but you're looking for a new ISP, several different Web sites offer lists of ISPs that you can switch to. Check the Resource Center at the end of this book for some of them.

Setting Up Your Internet Connection

Whatever ISP you choose, you need to enter some information so that the connecting software knows what to do. If you own a computer bought in the last few years, the odds are pretty good that you already have not only a modem but more than one set of software for connecting to the Net. PCs running Windows 95 and later have built-in networking facilities. Macintoshes and computers running UNIX have always had this capability.

The software of AOL or similar online services automatically walks you through the process of setting up your connection. Typically, the software asks you what city or area code you're connecting from. Next, the software either presents you with a listing of telephone numbers used for connection to that service or the software dials a toll-free number to access such a listing. You need to choose a phone number (and usually a second number for backup as well). Different phone numbers exist for different modem speeds, so you need to know your modem speed in order to decide which one to use.

The phone number or numbers you choose may be automatically entered in your software, or you may have to write them down and then type them in when asked to do so. In either case, writing them down and keeping them in a safe place is a good idea. Millions of things can go wrong with computers, and having a hard copy of vital information never hurts.

If you have call waiting on the phone line that you're using for your modem, your connection may be disrupted if someone calls and beeps through. To avoid this disruption, make sure that you add *70 at the beginning of the phone number so that call waiting is disabled whenever you connect.

Things can get a bit more complex if you're using a local ISP instead of a national online service. In this case, you need to have more information, but don't worry. Your ISP provides you with everything you need, and their technical support people are glad to walk you through the setup procedure on the phone. If they're not, they're not worth dealing with, and finding that out before you get started is a good idea.

Typically, you need to enter some or all of the following information:

- Telephone number of the Internet server
- Type of server (usually PPP)
- Network protocol (TCP/IP for Internet connections)
- IP address (usually not needed — most addresses are assigned dynamically, not permanently)
- DNS server address
- Gateway address

Don't let any of this intimidate you. It sounds a lot more complex than it is, and you don't need to even begin to understand how any of it works. All you have to do is punch in the information that the tech support folks (or the documentation) tell you to.

Write down all the information the tech support folks give you. You never know when you may need to reinput that information, and doing so can save you another call to your ISP's tech support.

Also, many local ISPs provide automated setup software similar to the national online services. But if they don't, the 15 or 20 minutes you take to get set up with them is worth the effort. You have access to a much greater range of Internet software options with a regular ISP. The major online services, such as AOL, supply their own software, and you may not get all the features you can get with a regular ISP's wider choice of programs.

CHAPTER 2
USING E-MAIL

IN THIS CHAPTER

- Understanding e-mail
- Using emoticons
- Coping with spam
- Joining mailing lists

One of the biggest benefits to getting on the Internet is that you can send messages electronically. While a regular letter takes days to get somewhere, electronic mail (or *e-mail*) flashes across the country or around the world in mere seconds. E-mail is literally faster than a speeding bullet and a whole lot cheaper than long-distance phone calls. No wonder people who use e-mail call regular mail *snail mail.* And no wonder e-mail is becoming the number one method of communication in the modern world.

This chapter fills you in on the basics of working with e-mail, from choosing an e-mail program to how to wink. And because even e-mail users are not immune to junk mail, we show you how to deal with that, too.

Understanding E-mail

In one respect, e-mail works just like snail mail. You type a message and then send it to a particular address where you know the message will get to a certain person. However, in the case of e-mail, the address is on the Internet instead of on a street. You don't have to mess with stamps and envelopes, and you're doing your part to save the trees — a pretty nice package, all in all.

Choosing an e-mail program

Deciding which program you use for e-mail is a personal decision. Most programs offer the same features, so the choice really boils down to which interface you like best and which program you find easiest to use.

Both of the major Web browsers (Microsoft Internet Explorer and Netscape Navigator, discussed in Chapter 3) come with their own e-mail programs (see Figure 2-1), and tons of standalone programs are available, as well. Why use a standalone e-mail program instead of your Web browser? Standalone e-mail programs are usually a lot smaller and take up considerably less computer resources to run.

Figure 2-1: Sending e-mail with Navigator.

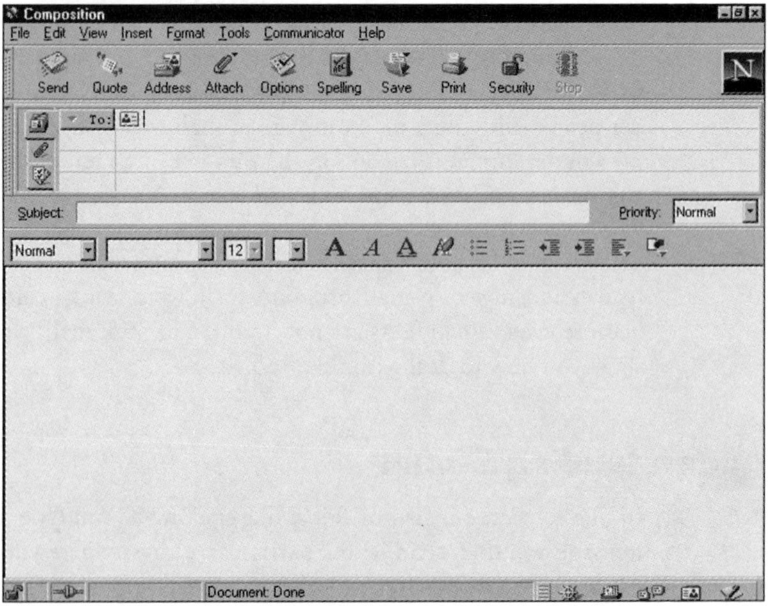

The Winfiles Web site (`www.winfiles.com`) contains a comprehensive listing of popular e-mail programs. Drop in and download a few.

Configuring an e-mail program

You need to know a few things to get your e-mail program working:

- **Your e-mail address:** This address is composed of your user name (the same one you log on to your ISP with) and your ISP's name, with an @ symbol between them (@ is pronounced "at"). So, if you're John Smith and your ISP is aeiouandy.com, your e-mail address is probably something like `jsmith@aeiouandy.com`.

- **Your password:** Like the user name, this password is the same one you use to log on to your ISP.

- **Your incoming mail server name:** Although you can use several types of mail servers, the most common is the POP (Post Office Protocol) server, so the address is probably something like `pop.aeiouandy.com`.

- **The outgoing mail server name:** This is usually an SMTP (Simple Mail Transfer Protocol) server, so the address is probably something like `smtp.aeiouandy.com`.

If you can, double-check with your ISP before you enter these settings into your e-mail program. Your ISP may use something a bit different. If these settings aren't working and you can't reach your ISP, try using `mail.aeiouandy.com` for both the incoming and outgoing mail servers (substituting your real ISP for `aeiouandy.com`, of course). If that doesn't work, wait until you can contact your ISP's tech support people.

Depending on the particular program, you can find these settings under menu choices such as Options, Tools, or Preferences. You're looking for a dialog box like the one in

Figure 2-2 that asks you to enter this sort of data. (You may have to use more than one dialog box to enter all the information.) After you find the correct dialog box, simply type in the information and then click OK.

Figure 2-2: Entering mail server data.

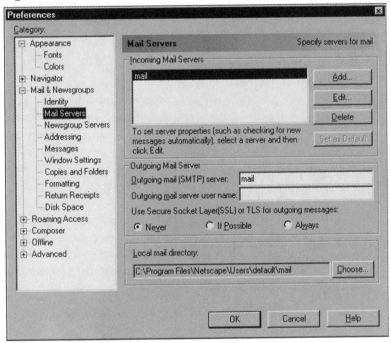

Creating and sending e-mail

To create a new message, you need a blank screen. Generally, you click an icon that has a little drawing of a blank page on it, or you may need to select something like File⇨New Message from the menu. After you get the blank screen, just type into it. Your program inserts your return address, but you need to tell it two things — where the message is going and what the subject is. For the first, you can either type in the e-mail address or — with most programs — select a recipient from an address book. You have to come up with subject on your own.

E-mail programs normally receive messages automatically. (You have to set your program's options to override automatic pickup to avoid it.) However, sending messages is another matter.

Practically every e-mail program enables you to send a message either by clicking an icon or by selecting a menu command, such as Message⇨Send. The exact details may vary from one program to another, but not by very much.

Take a few minutes to explore your program's icons. Place your mouse cursor over an icon and wait a moment. Most programs show a popup *help balloon* that describes the icon's function. Mac users must enable Help Balloons from the Help menu to get these little doodads to show up.

What do you do if you want to send more than words? That situation is where attachments come in. An *attachment* is a file that gets sent along with the message but isn't actually included within it. For example, you may want to send a digitized photo of your summer vacation to a friend. To do so, you have to tell the e-mail program to attach the file and where to find it. You can usually click an Attach button and just point to the filename on your hard drive (see Figure 2-3).

If you receive an attachment, don't open it unless you know who sent it. Programs containing viruses can be sent as attachments, but they can do no harm if you don't open them. Just delete the attachment. Although you can get a virus from any source, you should be more suspicious of sources you don't know.

Figure 2-3: Attaching a file.

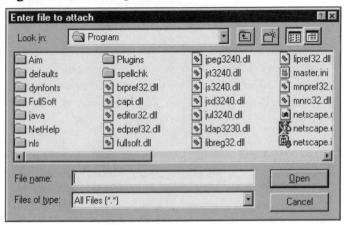

Adding sigs

Most people spice up their e-mail messages with a *sig* (short for *signature*). This isn't actually a signature, but it comes at the end of your messages, right where a signature would appear in a normal letter. Also called *tag lines,* these are short bits of text that are automatically added by your e-mail program whenever you send a message.

Sigs, similar to attachments, are separate files. But unlike attachments, sigs are included within the text of the message you're sending. They're plain-text files, and in many e-mail programs, you can enter them via a dialog box. If your e-mail program doesn't allow you to do this, just type your sig in a text editor and save it. You usually tell the program where to find the sig file in the same dialog box you use to identify the name of your mail server.

You can use sigs to say anything at all. You can even take sigs literally and have something like the following automatically appended to your messages:

Sincerely yours,

Me

Generally, though, people choose to include either a plug for their company that lists the URL of their main Web site or some short quotation that expresses their feelings. You may use the sig to list your address and phone number. If you're using a company e-mail account, you may not have any choice in the matter. Many corporations require you to use the sig to hold a disclaimer saying your opinions aren't necessarily those of the management.

If a major e-mail program exists that doesn't allow sigs, we've never seen it. A sig is one of the most common ways of expressing yourself, so don't pass up the opportunity.

Keep your sigs short. Nobody likes to get a message that's two lines long with a sig that takes up three pages. Although no hard and fast rule exists for it, four lines is an acceptable maximum.

Getting free e-mail accounts

One of the most popular things on the Net today is the free e-mail account. To get more visitors to their Web sites, many large sites are giving away free e-mail accounts. One company even lets you send e-mail without being on the Internet at all.

To check out your choices, drop in to Excite at `www.excite.com`, Juno at `www.juno.com`, Hotmail at `www.hotmail.com`, or practically any major site like a search engine or online community these days. Look for a link that says <u>free e-mail</u>, click it, and follow the instructions.

Using Emoticons and Abbreviations

E-mail users over the years have developed two conventions that can help you communicate accurately and quickly:

- A common set of *emoticons* (or emotional icons) to convey complex emotions with abbreviated symbols

- A somewhat standard set of abbreviations to convey common phrases using only the first letters of the words, more or less

Of course, if you don't understand what you're seeing in your messages, then these things don't help communication at all, so we show you how to interpret and use them.

Emoticons

One of the neat things you run across in e-mail is the *emoticon,* or *emotional icon* or *smiley.* Emoticons are ways to describe complex emotions with abbreviated symbols. E-mail doesn't permit us to see or hear the other person. So we miss out on all the visual cues that body language provides us in person, or the intentions we can read from the tone of voice in a telephone call. Telling from the words alone whether someone is being nasty or joking is often impossible.

Of course, the same problem exists in any written communication. Why emoticons evolved in e-mail but not in letters is an open question. Part of the answer lies in the slow speed of early modems and the limited storage capacities of early computers. While you can ramble on and explain every nuance of your meaning in a normal letter, early e-mail messages had to be extremely short and cut right to the point. Another contributing factor was probably that the first users of e-mail were scientists and engineers who were used to thinking and communicating in symbolic ways.

Even a simple statement from your boss, such as "I can't back this idea" can have several interpretations. From the written words alone, you can't tell if she's barking angrily or reluctantly backing off from what she thinks is a good concept.

You just can't tell for sure if you've made a good impression or if you're about to be fired.

So, just as someone would say "Smile when you say that" in the old westerns, someone, somewhere along the line, started making up human faces to go into e-mail messages. These emoticons are composed of the various symbols that you find on the nonalphabetical keys of your keyboard. Viewed sideways, they show a cartoon-style vision of various facial expressions that explain the meaning of the sentence they follow. Most of them are limited to showing eyes, nose, and mouth, but some throw in eyebrows. Some people leave the nose out of it entirely because it doesn't contribute to expressing emotion. But most e-mailers leave it in because it helps the caricature look more like a human face. Table 2-1 shows some of the more common emoticons.

Table 2-1: Commonly Used Emoticons

Symbol	Meaning
:-)	Smile
:->	Big smile
:-(	Sadness
:-<	Extreme sadness
>:-(	Anger, displeasure
:-o	Surprise, shock, pain
>:-o	Shouting
;-)	Wink

So, you may use them in sentences like the following:

Boy, you sure didn't earn your money. ;-)

He left you? :-o

I can't make i°t to the party. :-(

In the first example, the wink turns what would otherwise sound like an insult into a joke meaning the opposite of the actual words. In the second, shock is expressed, and in the third, sadness.

An almost endless variety of emoticons exist, and people invent more of them all the time. Some emoticons are pretty obscure and need to be explained before the intention is clear, like the man with styled hair smoking a pipe — 8:-P — but the best ones are obvious at a glance.

Abbreviations

Similar to emoticons, abbreviations evolved back when every byte had to be counted. By using abbreviations, you can make a long message much shorter. A shorter message takes less time to transmit and less room on the tiny storage devices of the early days of computing. (We remember being thrilled when we upgraded to that new, massive 10MB hard drive, and we still have a 300 bps modem lying around somewhere.) Another function of abbreviations is simply to avoid typing common phrases.

Abbreviations may no longer serve their original purpose. But they're still commonly used, not only in e-mail, but also in chat rooms and newsgroups. And new abbreviations are still being invented. Some of them show their later origins, such as afk, meaning "away from keyboard." That one clearly evolved from live online chats rather than the early days of e-mail, because only people on live need to know what you're doing at the moment.

Table 2-2 shows some of the more common abbreviations:

Table 2-2: Commonly Used Abbreviations

Abbreviation	Meaning
afk	Away from keyboard
brb	Be right back
btw	By the way
gmta	Great minds think alike
imho	In my humble opinion
lol	Laughing out loud
ltns	Long time no see
rotfl	Rolling on the floor laughing
tia	Thanks in advance
ttfn	Ta ta for now
ttyl	Talk to you later

Abbreviations have many variations. The abbreviation imho, for example, may show up as only *imo* (in my opinion) or *imnsho* (in my not-so-humble opinion), and rotfl may simply be *rotf* (rolling on the floor). Some abbreviations have evolved into words with their own peculiar structure. For example, lol can be turned into *lolol* or *lololol*, which have no real meaning as abbreviations but do emphasize that you're laughing really loud.

Coping with Spam

Whether your daily mail from the mailbox in front of your house or the mailbox inside your computer, you're bound to find something that you don't want and haven't ask for. With snail mail, you call it "junk mail" and toss it into the trash can without opening it. With e-mail, you call it *spam*. And a great deal of anguish and anger about it exists on the Internet.

Why is unwanted e-mail called spam? Not because Internet folks don't like canned lunch meat. The term comes from an old skit from the British comedy troupe Monty Python, in which a restaurant served nothing but the product Spam. You could order Spam sandwiches, Spam and eggs, Spam and whatever, but nothing else at all. The people in the restaurant — a group of Vikings, actually, but what do you expect from Monty Python? — began to chant, "Spam, Spam, Spam, Spam," over and over again. When commercial e-mail first began to show up in vast quantities, it seemed as though it was all you could get from your mail server. Remembering the comedy routine, people began to call unsolicited commercial e-mail "spam."

Recognizing spam

Spam is usually easy to spot by the subject of the message. About 90 percent is some sort of get-rich-quick scheme, and typically you can find some mention of money or wealth in the subject line. Just in case you're actually tempted to send money to these people, remember that about the only way to get rich quick is to convince others that you know how they can get rich quick and then sucker them into sending you money. You're better off buying a lottery ticket or investing in a stock you picked at random than falling for one of these purported sure-fire plans for early retirement.

Spam isn't simply unsolicited e-mail. After all, if your best friend sends you a message, it's probably not one you solicited. In fact, you can't solicit e-mail without sending unsolicited e-mail yourself, unless you want to use the telephone or a snail mail letter to ask someone to send you a message via e-mail. Just trying to sort out this situation can make your head spin, and some of the arguments get pretty silly, but the simple fact is that almost all e-mail is unsolicited. Spam mostly comes from people trying to sell you something; these people may have no idea who you are or whether you'd be interested in their products. Some spammers send the message out to every single e-mail address they can get their hands on. Spam also includes messages from people or organizations trying to tell you the end of the world is near, save your soul from evil spirits infesting the Internet, spread urban legends (see Chapter 8), pass on chain letters, and the like.

Fighting spam

The best way to handle spam is the same way you handle physical junk mail — just toss it in the trash can without even looking at it. Pressing your Del key is faster than taking any sort of action against the spammer. However, if you're upset or angry about the spam or if the sender is being particularly obnoxious — such as the ones who send you the same message 87 times in a row — you have a few options:

- You can report the spam to your ISP. Send them a copy of the spam and tell them you're unhappy about it. You should address the complaint to the postmaster at your ISP — if your ISP is called aeiouandy.com, then you send your complaint to `postmaster@aeiouandy.com`.

- You can also notify the sender's ISP. In that case, you need to send your complaint to a special address called *abuse*. Most ISPs have that address set up specifically for the purpose of handling such complaints. If the spammer is using an ISP called spammer.com, you send your complaint to `abuse@spammer.com`. If that special mailbox isn't set up, and you get the mail returned as undeliverable, you can always try sending your complaint to `postmaster@spammer.com` instead. Either way, you should reach someone who can deal with the problem.

- Most ISPs prohibit using their systems for sending spam. Some, regrettably, have another policy entirely and actually encourage spammers to use them. If the ISP is one of the responsible ones and follows the normal pattern,

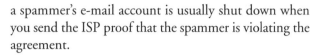

a spammer's e-mail account is usually shut down when you send the ISP proof that the spammer is violating the agreement.

■ You can stop many commercial e-mail messages by replying to them with the word *remove* in the subject line. In many cases, though, replying to spam that says you can be removed in this way has the opposite effect. Replying tells the spammers which e-mail addresses are still live and may actually increase your spam load.

Some ISPs go to extreme lengths in their attempts to fight spam. Our former ISP went so far as to install mail-filtering software that slowed the delivery speed of incoming and outgoing mail by about 2000 percent. This software made our nice, fast modem about as useful as an antique. The ISP also rigged their system so that none of their users could access their remote e-mail accounts, thus effectively cutting off thousands of innocent people from full access to the Internet while possibly inconveniencing two or three spammers. The result of this idiotic crusade was — you guessed it — that we still got tons of spam in our mailbox.

Opting in to newsletters

A kind of commercial e-mail is practiced by responsible (and smart) merchants on the Internet. This kind of e-mail is called *opt-in* e-mail, which means that you request, or exercise the option, to become a recipient of their mailings. In some cases, you don't get anything for your trouble but a bunch of garbage in your mailbox. But several outfits do provide worthwhile and informative newsletters along with their sales pitches.

One of the finer examples of opt-in e-mail is the PC Shopping Planet newsletter. You can opt-in by submitting your e-mail address in the form at the bottom of the Web page at `www.shoppingplanet.com`. (No, we don't get a percentage — we just appreciate good work when we see it.) If you don't like what you get after you opt-in to someone's newsletter, getting yourself removed from the list is easy. Companies that practice this kind of approach are very good about keeping their subscribers happy.

Before you make a complaint about someone you think is a spammer, make sure that you didn't choose to opt-in to their mailings a long time ago and have forgotten about doing so.

Exploring Mailing Lists

On the Internet, *mailing list* doesn't mean the same thing as it does with snail mail. Instead of a group of addresses sold to anyone who wants to send mail to the addressees, an Internet mailing list means a discussion group that's conducted via e-mail. Although such groups today are run by specialized software, they originated with one person sending out a message simultaneously to several others who wanted to discuss a subject. They used a plain e-mail program to send to many e-mail addresses at once, and all those addresses were compiled in a list. Calling such a group a mailing list is an unfortunate choice of words, but the term is here to stay.

Joining mailing lists

Discussion groups (lists) exist on just about every topic you can imagine. If you're a cat lover, you can join a list on cats; if you want to keep up-to-date on the latest developments in computing, a list exists for just about every technology. How do you find out about these lists? Some lists have their own Web sites that you can find through the search engines, while others you just trip over or find by word of mouth.

A great source of mailing lists is PAML (Publicly Available Mailing Lists), a Web site dedicated to keeping track of all the lists that they can find. At this site, you can search by topic or browse through an alphabetical listing and learn all about the lists. You can find PAML's Web site (see Figure 2-4) at www.neosoft.com/internet/paml. Another, similar site is called Liszt (no, that's not a typo), and you can find their Web site at www.liszt.com.

Figure 2-4: The PAML Web site.

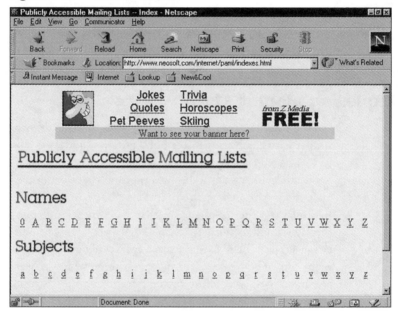

When you find a list that you want to try, you can join by sending an e-mail message to the subscription address. Usually, a message with only the word *subscribe* and the name of the list will suffice, although you do find some variations such as *join*. Your subscription request is processed, either by software or a human, and your e-mail address is added to the subscriber base. If the request is processed by software, you should receive confirmation that you've joined pretty quickly, often within a couple of minutes. If your request is approved by a person, you may have to wait for a few days, especially if a weekend and/or holiday intervenes.

After you become a subscriber, and if the list is a busy one, your mailbox starts filling up with messages on your favorite topic in no time. If the list is not so busy, a few messages may trickle in from time to time.

If you join a list on a fascinating topic but with very little traffic, try sending some messages to the list to break the ice and get a conversation going.

Mailing lists work like this: After you join, you send a message on the topic to a central e-mail address. At that address, a program called a *listserver* automatically relays a copy of the message to all the other members' e-mail addresses.

Many mailing lists maintain an archive of old messages. Often, you can get valuable information by searching through them. Almost all mailing lists also have a list of Frequently Asked Questions (FAQ) that you can benefit from.

Mailing list netiquette

That strange word *netiquette* is short for Internet etiquette, and nothing much is mysterious about it. You get along on the Net the same way you do off it — keep other people's feelings in mind, and you can't go too wrong.

Here are a few general netiquette guidelines:

- The main thing is to restrain your emotions. Getting excited over something or having a strong opinion is okay, but you absolutely have to keep your on-list behavior within certain boundaries. If someone posts a message on the list saying something that you think is wrong, nothing is wrong with replying to say why you don't agree and laying out a counter-argument.

- If you let yourself get carried away and get into personal attacks, though, you're doing more damage to the list than any kind of legitimate disagreement can do. A message carrying anger and insults instead of worthwhile content is called a *flame,* and if everyone gives vent to their own responses to it, the list can quickly devolve into a *flame war,* which is an exchange of insults. A mailing list is only as good as its content, so do everything you can to keep that content at a good level.

■ Most mailing lists don't want you to send attachments with your messages. Sending out multiple copies of the attachment takes up a lot of their server's resources, and many of their subscribers may not want the attachment, anyway.

If you have something you want to share, post it on your own Web site and then send a message to the list telling the other subscribers where to find it if they want.

■ When quoting a message for reply, you don't have to quote the whole thing. In your reply, delete all the quoted parts that you're not responding to and leave only the pertinent parts intact. This saves time for the reader and makes understanding what you mean easier. If you need to clarify that you're doing this, you can add the word *snip* in brackets, like this: [snip]. This tells anyone reading the message that you edited the quoted part and shows them where you snipped out the edited parts.

■ Don't ever send a reply to a message on a list just saying "Me, too." If you don't have anything to contribute except for the fact that you agree, you don't have anything to contribute at all.

■ If you're going on vacation and you set your e-mail program to automatically respond to incoming messages with an announcement to that effect, make sure that you unsubscribe from all your mailing lists first. Otherwise, while you're enjoying yourself on the beach, the other list subscribers will be cursing you for sending a vacation reply to every message that gets posted to the list.

■ Don't join a list if you disagree with its premise. These are largely social or work groups, and nobody on a Linux list wants to hear you talk about how great you think Windows is, or vice versa. Disagreeing is one thing, but crashing the party when you have nothing to contribute is considered rude.

■ For the same reason, stay on the topic — don't suddenly start talking about gun control on a mailing list that's dedicated to mapmaking or about your favorite recipes on a list that's about stamp collecting. Most list owners tolerate a little bit of digression, but that's not the list's purpose.

■ Different mailing lists have varying policies about accepting messages promoting commercial products. If you have something to sell that you think may interest the members of the list, check with the list owner before you post a message about the product. If you do find that you can post such a message, keep it free of hype and just state clearly what the product does, how much it costs, and where to get it.

Warning

If you're disruptive or violate the rules of the mailing list, the list owner/manager has the right to remove you from the subscriber base.

Almost every mailing list sends you a set of rules when you first join, and good list owners make sure they post the rules from time to time, just in case anyone's forgotten them. Familiarize yourself with the rules and stick to them. They're not usually hard to abide by and generally ask you to be polite and stick to the list's subject matter.

CHAPTER 3

BROWSING THE WEB

IN THIS CHAPTER

- Understanding the World Wide Web
- Picking a Web browser
- Choosing your home page
- Finding Web sites

E-mail may be the most common use of the Internet. The most fun, though, is browsing the World Wide Web. The Web is filled with color and sound, in addition to being useful. And people seem to naturally take to that glitzy multimedia experience. In this chapter, you find out about the kind of software you need to *browse the Web* (the programs used to do this are called *browsers*). Also, you get the basics you need to enjoy the journey. We show you how to set your home page, how to find your way back to Web sites you like, and how to search through the vast number of Web pages to find the ones you want to look at.

Understanding the World Wide Web

The *World Wide Web* is a collection of separate documents called *Web pages* that are linked together. The software that enables you to view these documents and explore the links interconnecting them is called a *Web browser,* or just *browser* for short. When you follow a link from one page to the next, the linked page loads into the browser in place of the previous page.

Following links

Links are typically underlined, blue-colored text. You activate them by clicking them with a mouse. Certain specialized programs, such as those for the visually disabled, handle links differently and activate the links in various manners.

Remember

Links can also be images instead of text. In this case, the images are usually outlined with a blue border.

The color of a link changes after you visit it. Your Web browser remembers where you go and changes the link color from blue to red, so that you know where you've already been. By blazing a trail for you, this feature is useful in two ways: You can retrace your steps if you want to or you can avoid covering the same turf if you want to go somewhere new.

Going back and forth

Every link is a two-way street, and your Web browser keeps track of where you've been and what links you followed to get there. Two buttons — Back and Forward — on the browser toolbar enable you to run back and forth along the link pathway without having to manually retrace your steps. However, the Back and Forward buttons only work during a particular browsing session. Whenever you shut down your Web browser and then start it up again, you begin a new link track. That's why the two buttons don't do anything at all when you first start your browser. You have to visit a Web page in order to have somewhere to go back to.

Links have two ends called *anchors*. The end you come from is the *source anchor,* and the end you go to is the *destination anchor*. If you're using the Back and Forward buttons, a particular Web page can be the destination anchor at one moment and suddenly become the source anchor the next moment — it's all relative, depending on the direction you're going.

The URL of the page that you're viewing shows up in the small white area (called the *address box*) at the top of your Web browser. When following links, you normally don't have to concern yourself with the address box because the process is completely automatic. You just click a link and arrive at the Web page at the other end of that link. However, you sometimes do want to manually enter a URL in the address box. Doing so can be very useful whenever you find Web addresses from many sources that aren't on the Web, such as in television commercials or on business cards.

Picking a Web Browser

Currently, two major Web browsers exist on the market. Netscape Navigator is available either as a stand-alone program or as a part of the suite of programs called Netscape Communicator. Microsoft Internet Explorer comes bundled with Windows. Although both browsers are similar in purpose, appearance, and function, each has its own quirks and capabilities. Depending on your personal preferences, either one may work better for you. Many people use them both, and if you have the space on your hard drive, that's probably the best answer.

Some Web sites are specifically designed to take advantage of the particular features of one Web browser. To fully experience these sites, you need to have that browser on your system.

Netscape Navigator

Netscape Navigator (see Figure 3-1) was the first commercially successful Web browser. It was built on the model of the earlier Mosaic browser, which many people at Netscape had worked on. Navigator incorporated a number of improvements in speed, efficiency, and features. Navigator has gone through many upgrades since then, and it's still the most intuitive and easy to use of the major browsers.

Figure 3-1: Netscape Navigator.

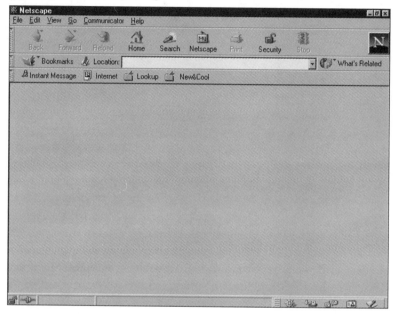

You can download Navigator from the Netscape Web site at `www.netscape.com`.

Microsoft Internet Explorer

Belatedly realizing that it had made a huge mistake in thinking that the Internet wasn't all that important, Microsoft scrambled to come up with Internet Explorer (see Figure 3-2) as its answer to Navigator. Like Navigator, Internet Explorer was based on the earlier Mosaic browser.

Figure 3-2: Internet Explorer.

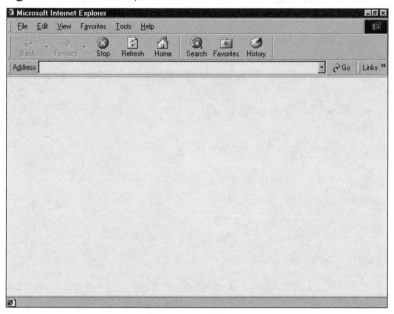

If you have Windows, you probably have Internet Explorer; Microsoft includes it. If you deleted it, you can still get it from the Microsoft Web site at www.microsoft.com.

 Having the latest version of a Web browser is always best. Frequently check the software publisher's Web site to see if your browser is up-to-date.

Other Web browsers

Although Netscape and Microsoft account for more than 90 percent of the Web browser market, some doggedly determined competitors still exist. If you want to try some of their browsers, you can download a few of them from the sites in Table 3-1.

Table 3-1: Web Browsers

Browser	Web site
Amaya	`www.w3.org/Amaya/User/BinDist`
Arachne	`http://xch.arachne.cz`
HotJava	`http://java.sun.com/products/hotjava`
Opera	`www.operasoftware.com`

Choosing Your Home Page

The phrase *home page* has two meanings. One is a Web page that you design to express or showcase your own personal interests. For example, you may include pictures of your children or links to other Web sites that deal with your favorite hobby. The other, somewhat more practical meaning is the page that automatically opens when you start your Web browser.

The latter serves as a valuable point of entry for you. The whole purpose of getting on the Web is to move from page to page along the vast maze of interconnected links. So the home page, as your starting point, should enable you to jump easily into the rest of the Web.

When you first install any Web browser, the home page is already set. Invariably, your first home page is the Web page of the people who make the browser. If you find their home page useful as an entry point to the World Wide Web, you can leave it alone. On the other hand, you can use any Web page as your home page, so you have a lot of latitude with tens of millions of Web pages from which to choose.

If you're inclined to create Web pages, you can merge the two meanings of *home page* and create your own page that you set to appear first in your Web browser. In this case, you can set up a page that has links to pages of special interest to you.

For example, if you're interested in stocks and bonds, you can include links to financial news sites such as `http://cnnfn.com`, various stock exchanges, and so forth.

As an alternative, you can choose from among the thousands of different points of entry that specialize in being portals to the Web. Any of the major search engines and Internet indexes fit this category. See the "Finding Web Sites" section later in this chapter. Or you may be purely fanatical about one topic. In that case, you can shop around and find your favorite page of links to resources specializing in that topic.

Although the actual process for setting your home page varies a bit from one Web browser to another, the basic principle is the same. We show you how to do so in both of the two major Web browsers.

Setting a home page in Navigator

To set your home page in Netscape Navigator, follow these steps:

1. Select Edit⟶Preferences from the Navigator menu bar. The Preferences dialog box appears, as shown in Figure 3-3.

2. Under Category in the panel on the left, select Navigator.

3. Click the Home Page radio button in the top panel under Navigator starts with. You can also choose to start with a blank page or with the last page you visited. If you start with a blank page, however, you have to manually type in the URL of any page you want to go to or choose a page from your bookmarks (see "Bookmarking Pages" later in this chapter).

4. Under Home page in the next panel, type the URL of the page that you want to use as your home page. As an alternative, click the Browse button to select a file on your own computer as your home page.

Figure 3-3:   The Navigator Preferences dialog box.

Preferences	☒

Category:

- Appearance
  - Fonts
  - Colors
- Navigator
  - Languages
  - Applications
  - Smart Browsing
- Mail & Newsgroups
- Roaming Access
- Composer
- Offline
- Advanced

Navigator   Specify the home page location

Navigator starts with

- ○ Blank page
- ◉ Home page
- ○ Last page visited

Home page

Clicking the Home button will take you to this page.

Location: http://www.linkfinder.com/index.html

[Use Current Page]   [Browse...]

History

History is a list of the pages you have previously visited.

Pages in history expire after: 9 days   [Clear History]

Location Bar History

Clear the list of sites on the location bar: [Clear Location Bar]

[OK]   [Cancel]   [Help]

5. Click OK to complete the process.

You can click the Use Current Page button to automatically enter the URL of the page currently displayed in your browser.

Setting a home page in Internet Explorer

To set your home page in Internet Explorer, follow these steps:

1. Select Tools⇨Internet Options from the Microsoft Internet Explorer menu bar. (For a version of Internet Explorer prior to Version 5.0, the menu choice is View⇨Internet Options.) The Internet Options dialog box appears.

2. Select the General tab shown in Figure 3-4.

Figure 3-4: The Internet Explorer Internet Options dialog box.

Internet Options	? X

General | Security | Content | Connections | Programs | Advanced |

┌─ Home page ──────────────────────────────────
│ 🏠 You can change which page to use for your home page.
│   Add_r_ess: [http://www.linkfinder.com/]
│   [Use _C_urrent] [Use _D_efault] [Use _B_lank]

┌─ Temporary Internet files ───────────────────
│ 📁 Pages you view on the Internet are stored in a special folder
│   for quick viewing later.
│   [Delete _F_iles...] [_S_ettings...]

┌─ History ────────────────────────────────────
│ 🕒 The History folder contains links to pages you've visited for
│   quick access to recently viewed pages.
│   Days to _k_eep pages in history: [20 ⬍] [Clear _H_istory]

[C_o_lors...] [Fo_n_ts...] [_L_anguages...] [Acc_e_ssibility...]

[OK] [Cancel] [Apply]

3. In the Address text box in the top panel, type the URL of the page you want to use as your home page.

Tip

You can click the Use Current button to automatically enter the URL of the page currently displayed in your browser. Or you can click the Use Blank button to start with a blank page. The Use Default button sets the home page back to the Microsoft Web page.

4. Click OK to complete the process.

Bookmarking Web Pages

No matter where you are on the Web, you can return to your home page at any time simply by hitting your Home button. You can have only one home page, however, so how do you go back to other pages that you don't intend to make your home page? The same way you use a bookmark to let you go back to a page in a book. Furthermore, you can create as many bookmarks as you want in your Web browser.

Bookmarking pages in Navigator

To add a bookmark in Netscape Navigator, click the Bookmarks button in the Navigator toolbar and then click the Add Bookmark option in the drop-down menu that appears, as shown in Figure 3-5.

Figure 3-5:   Navigator bookmarks.

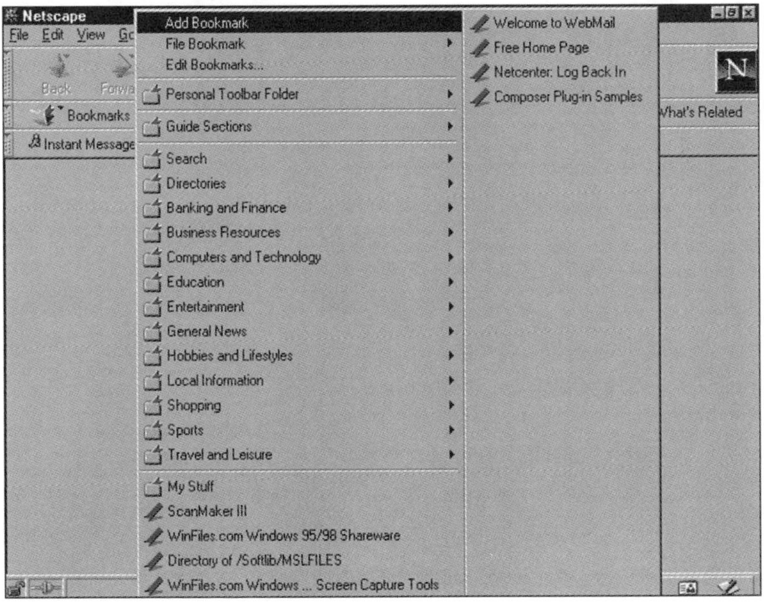

To return to that page later, click the Bookmarks button in the Navigator toolbar and then click the name of the Web page in the drop-down list.

Bookmarking pages in Internet Explorer

To add a bookmark in Internet Explorer, follow these steps:

1. Select Favorites⇨Add to Favorites from the Internet Explorer menu bar.

2. In the Add Favorite dialog box, shown in Figure 3-6, click OK.

Figure 3-6: Adding a bookmark.

To return to a bookmarked page later, click the Favorites button in the toolbar. A separate window appears containing a list of your bookmarks, as shown in Figure 3-7. Click the name of the site you want.

Figure 3-7:   Internet Explorer bookmarks.

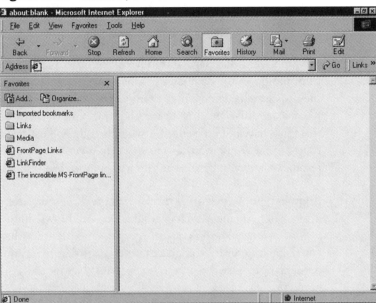

Searching for Web Sites

With the zillions of Web pages that cover every topic known to humanity, you can find out about anything that interests you. Or can you? In order to get to a Web page, you have to go to its address, and where are you going to get that?

Finding the right Web page is much worse than finding a needle in a haystack. Because Web page authorship is such an easy task, more and more pages crop up every second. Even as you read these words, the number of available Web pages is increasing.

Cataloging the Web

The task of cataloging all these Web pages is virtually impossible. Still, some Web sites manage to collect a great deal of information on the addresses and topics of Web pages. Some of these sites utilize programs called *robots* to search the World Wide Web. The robots surf to a Web page, add the address of the page and the words on it into a database, then follow the links from that page and move on to other pages. The information in the database then becomes searchable, and the site's search engine builds a temporary Web page of links to the pages that match your search terms. Oddly, many of these sites have put little effort into building the sophisticated type of search engine that consistently gives worthwhile responses, and you have to put up with a lot of bad results.

Another type of directory is the *Internet index*. This directory is made of permanent Web pages that you can browse in the normal manner. The links are categorized, and you find what you're looking for by going to the Web page that covers the particular category that interests you. Most Net indexes also have some sort of search capacity similar to the database sites, thus giving you the ability to use whichever approach you're comfortable with. Table 3-2 gives the URLs of several Web directory sites.

Table 3-2: Web Directories

Site	URL
Excite	www.excite.com
GoTo.com	www.goto.com
HotBot	www.hotbot.com
LinkFinder	www.linkfinder.com
SavvySearch	www.savvysearch.com
Snap	www.snap.com
Yahoo!	www.yahoo.com

Many smaller, more specialized Web sites catalog a large number of links to a very limited and specific subject. Generally, these sites are put together by an individual with an intense interest in the topic. The sites are usually nothing more than the results of a search performed at a large directory site, but they're fast and easy to use.

The great problem with any type of Web links directory is that things change so quickly. As a result, much of the information is outdated. Web pages that existed yesterday are gone tomorrow. So one of the main tasks of any directory site administrator is to keep the bad links cleaned out. Unfortunately, many administrators don't even try to do this. Still, even with the inevitable frustration of following up the occasional dead link, no better way exists to find your way around the World Wide Web than taking advantage of a site in which someone else has already done most of the surfing for you.

Using search engines

Regardless of the method a directory site uses to amass its information on Web pages, the search process you follow at a catalog site is pretty much the same. Every search engine has a text box into which you enter the terms you want to search for, as shown in Figure 3-8.

Picking the right search terms (or keywords, as they're sometimes called) is the heart of the art of searching, and that's your job. The brains of it fall under the heading of Boolean logic, which is the job of the search engine. Don't let that term intimidate you, by the way — it's just a way of specifying a search term and is named after a guy named Boole. Here is where the software gives you a helping hand.

Figure 3-8: A search form.

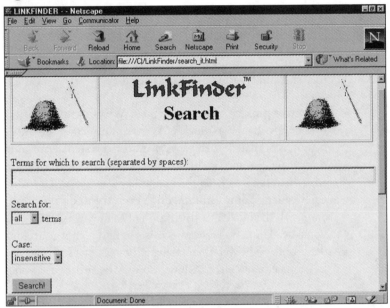

Suppose, for example, that you want to search for information on President Kennedy. You may use **JFK** as your search term. However, with all the different buildings, monuments, and organizations named after him, you'll probably get a lot of results that aren't what you're looking for. The trick is to narrow your search, which is where Boolean logic comes in.

Boolean logic offers three possibilities in Web searching:

■ Find this term *and* that term.

■ Find this term *or* that term.

■ Find this term but *not* that term.

You can narrow the search by adding more terms and specifying how the search engine handles them. For that, you use Boolean operators that correspond to the three possibilities in the list above — AND, OR, and NOT. Instead of just typing **JFK,** try **JFK AND Massachusetts** or use **JFK AND senator AND president.** With each additional *AND* you use, you further limit the number of possible responses, because the search results have to include all the search terms you specify. Most search engines by default assume that you intend to use *AND*, so you usually don't have to do anything but list a bunch of search terms in a row. In that case, typing the search term **JFK senator president** is equivalent to typing **JFK AND senator AND president.**

Boolean operators have to be in capital letters so the search engine knows they're not just common words.

On the other hand, if you want to broaden the search, thus increasing the number of possible responses from the search engine, you use the *OR* operator. For example, you can type **JFK OR Onassis** to find Web pages that have information on either of Jackie Kennedy's famous husbands. To illustrate the difference in the way these two operators work, if you type **JFK AND Onassis** instead, the search results include only Web pages that contain information on both of them.

To exclude a term from the search results, you use the *NOT* operator. For example, suppose you want to find everything you can about President Kennedy but want no information at all about his First Lady. So you type **JFK NOT Jackie.**

Some search engines require you to use *AND NOT* or *BUT NOT* instead of just plain *NOT.* Check the search engine's help page, just to be sure.

The real power of Boolean operators comes from combining them. You can use any or all of them in a single search phrase. If you want to know everything about Jackie Kennedy before she married Onassis, for example, you can try **Jackie AND Kennedy NOT Onassis.** When using complex groupings, use parentheses to make sure that the search engine understands your intentions. For example, you can try to cover all the bases, getting more specific in the search, by using both the formal and informal versions of her first name, as well as both her maiden name and her married name during the Kennedy years. This more specific approach may look like this: **(Jackie OR Jacqueline) AND (Bouvier OR Kennedy) NOT Onassis.** The parentheses clarify your meaning and help to make sure that you get what you're looking for.

Remember

If you don't use parentheses to group search terms, the Boolean operators are automatically interpreted from left to right, which may or may not give you the results you're looking for.

Sometimes, you want to look for a particular phrase instead of individual words. To tell this to a search engine, just type the search terms in quotation marks, as in **"John Kennedy"**. This limits the search results to only those Web pages that have that exact combination of words — in that exact order. Pages that have the same words, but not in that order, won't be matches for that search. If you run the same search terms, but don't use the quotation marks — as in **John Kennedy** — you find every Web page in the search engine's database that contains the name John and the name Kennedy. Because both of them are common names, you end up getting back an awful lot of personnel and membership directories as search results. And you probably receive more pages than you can browse through in a year. Get as specific as possible when choosing the search phrase, such as typing **"John Fitzgerald Kennedy"**. A lot of people are named after such a famous person, so you're better off using **"President John Fitzgerald Kennedy"**.

All this may seem a bit intimidating at first glance, but you quickly find that it becomes second nature. These searching skills can help you immeasurably when you want to find something on the Web.

CHAPTER 4
GETTING THE GOODIES

IN THIS CHAPTER

- Downloading free files
- Getting expert advice
- Keeping up with the news
- Reading e-zines

The World Wide Web is chock full of goodies that you can grab for nothing (or next to nothing). You can find free graphics, free programs, free advice, and free magazines. You can spend the rest of your life just trying to keep up with it all.

In this chapter, you learn how to get programs and graphics by just asking — simply click a link and the file downloads to your computer. You can get all the latest news anytime, day or night, and your favorite magazines are probably online for you to read.

Downloading Free Files

Getting your hands on free software is much easier these days. You just use your Web browser to locate and download the files. After you browse to a Web page that contains the link to the files, you just click the link and then decide which folder on your system to store the software in.

 Downloadable files are usually compressed so that they transmit faster. The most common method is the *zipped* file, which requires a program such as PKZIP, WinZip, or another compatible program to uncompress the file.

Exploring shareware, freeware, and demos

Everyone's familiar with the kind of software that you buy in a box from the shelf of a computer or office supply store. However, small software publishers find competing with the marketing muscle of big companies difficult. As a result, the small publishers evolved a unique marketing approach of their own called *shareware*.

Shareware programs are often just as good and sophisticated as their better known commercial counterparts, but you can get them on a "try-before-you-buy" basis. Shareware is a fully functional copy, not some demo version of the product that shows a few features without actually allowing you to use it.

Shareware has a tremendous appeal for the buyer. After all, if you plop down hundreds of dollars for regular software in a store and then don't like the program, returning it is almost impossible. When you try shareware, you download the program without paying for it, play with it or work with it, and then decide whether you like it and whether it's worth parting with your money. Shareware is usually a lot less expensive than normal commercial software, because the publisher doesn't have to pay for all that advertising and packaging.

Recognizing the tremendous appeal of shareware to the buying public, the big software companies often take a small step toward the shareware marketing approach. Some of them even embrace the shareware concept in addition to their normal marketing channels. For example, you can purchase Norton AntiVirus software in a packaged version from a store or download it via the Internet on a trial basis.

Another even better thing is *freeware*. This software is just what it sounds like — free. Of course, you get a really wild variation in the quality of freeware. Because the authors aren't competing in the commercial marketplace, nothing spurs them to add all the bells and whistles that you find in similar shareware programs. As a result, much freeware isn't worth the price. However, you can find some surprising exceptions, and some freeware is easily on a par with commercial programs. Even when the freeware program isn't on a par with commercial programs, you may still find it useful. Lots of freeware consists of short, simple little programs that solve a particular need. If you have that need, then you bless the author.

Unfortunately, some freely distributed software is *crippleware*. That term refers to demonstration software that's rigged not to work right. Most shareware programs have some sort of limitation on them, but not on their functionality. Generally, shareware only works for a limited time, perhaps 30 days, or only allows you to launch the program a certain number of times. Some shareware programs won't work after the limit is reached and others start showing a nag screen asking you to pay up. However, shareware never limits your ability to use the program during the trial period. Crippleware is different. Crippleware never works; it's only a glorified demo. The crippleware program's limitations may include not allowing you to save your work or preventing you from printing your work. The bottom line is that you should always read the author's ReadMe file to determine how the software works, what the limitations are during the evaluation period, and how to ask questions of the author if you're unsure of anything.

Downloading by the bushel

In addition to the Web sites where particular software publishers or private authors offer their own products for you to download, tons of sites offer for downloading just about any kind of software you can imagine (see Figure 4-1, the Jumbo home page.) Table 4-1 shows some of the more popular ones:

Figure 4-1: The Jumbo home page.

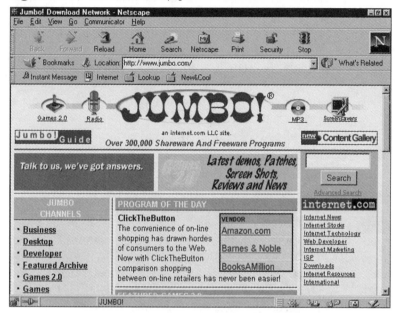

Table 4-1: Shareware Download Sites

Web site	URL
Download.com	www.download.com
Freeware	www.freewarehome.com
Jumbo	www.jumbo.com
Softseek	www.softseek.com
Topsoft	www.topsoft.com
WebAttack	www.webattack.com
Winfiles	www.winfiles.com

Beefing up your own site

If you have a site on the World Wide Web — and if you
don't, you will, trust us on this — you probably love all the
things that you can get for your site without paying a dime.

Do you want to add a daily comic strip that looks like the strips you see in the newspapers? Try Erik Sansom's charming Toy Trunk Railroad, shown in Figure 4-2, at `www.toytrunkrailroad.com`.

Figure 4-2:   Toy Trunk Railroad.

Do you want to include on your site all the fancy bells and whistles that make it really stand out? You can get thousands of Web site add-ons for free. You can easily add headline tickers or even entire news pages. Just drop in at 7am.com at `http://7am.com` and sign up for either service.

Table 4-2 gives the URLs for sites that give away freebies that you can use to improve your Web site.

Table 4-2: Sites with Freebies

Web site	URL
Animated Banner Maker	`www.mediabuilder.com/abm.html`
CGI Free	`www.cgi-free.com`
Dynamic Drive DHTML	`http://dynamicdrive.com`
FreeCode	`www.freecode.com`
JavaScripts.com	`www.javascripts.com`
Matt's Script Archive	`www.worldwidemart.com/scripts`
New Joke of the Day	`http://newjoke.com/home.htm`

Getting Expert Advice

One of the truly great things about the Internet is that with it you can reach just about any expert. Whatever topic you need to research, you're bound to find several experts who are willing to answer your questions.

Finding experts

Finding expert advice on topics such as building Web pages is easy. After all, every site on the Web has a creator, and all of them have their two cents worth to put in. If you want something more official, you can always drop in to HTML Tutorials (`www.htmlgoodies.com/tutors`) or the Web Developers Virtual Library (`www.wdvl.com`). But what if you want information on something like plasma physics or need to find out about the typical rainfall patterns in Tierra del Fuego?

You can start at Experts.com (`www.experts.com`), which lists people in a wide variety of fields from law to art. Or you can go to a search site, perform a search of the subject matter, and then look on those Web sites to see if they provide e-mail addresses for the experts.

Questioning experts

Many experts fit the categories of expert witnesses or consultants, which means that they make a living selling their knowledge. If you're on a tight budget, be aware that you're not likely to get much free assistance from people in these categories. So you may want to check their Web sites for references to fees.

Usually, you're far better off seeking people who work daily in the field or who teach the subject at a major university. Nonprofit organizations, specialized libraries, and other similar institutions also offer fertile fields for locating cooperative experts.

When you do find someone who looks as though he or she may be able to help, keep in mind that the person has plenty of things to do other than just answer your questions. Even if he or she has a Web page inviting questions, keep your queries short and to the point. Make sure that you ask all the questions for which you need answers and only those questions. Following these guidelines can help you avoid wasting the expert's precious time because, hopefully, you will only need one e-mail exchange.

Also, being polite never hurts. Explain briefly why you need the answers. Remember, you're writing to a human being, not just an e-mail address. Like anyone else, the expert enjoys knowing the people he or she is dealing with and knowing that you appreciate the help. Don't forget to drop the person a line of thanks.

Keeping Up with the News

Many news sites exist on the World Wide Web. Some sites belong to major international organizations such as CNN (see Figure 4-3) that provide general news to the world. Others belong to local newspapers with a Web presence. Still others belong to local radio and television stations that make their regular news broadcasts available on the Web. (For more information, see Chapter 7.) Even those organizations that don't make their regular reports available usually have some sort of Web site that lets you keep up with local developments.

If you visit the same news site frequently, and the news doesn't seem to change at all, your Web browser may be showing you an old version of the page that's kept in the *cache* (a part of your hard drive that your browser sets aside to keep copies of recently visited sites). Click the Reload (or Refresh) button in your browser's toolbar to force the page to load the most recent version.

Figure 4-3:   The CNN Web site.

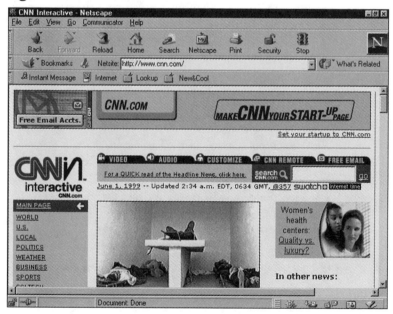

Table 4-3 shows some of the bigger news sites on the World
Wide Web:

Table 4-3: News Sites on the Web

Web site	*URL*
CNN	`www.cnn.com`
London Times	`www.londontimes.com`
Los Angeles Times	`www.latimes.com`
MSNBC	`www.msnbc.com`
New York Times	`www.nytimes.com`
Newsday	`www.newsday.com`
Newsweek	`www.newsweek.com`
Time	`http://cgi.pathfinder.com/time`
Washington Post	`www.washingtonpost.com`

Following sports

What can you do? You live in one city, but your favorite team
plays in another. Every sports fan knows how hard it can be
to keep up–to-date with a distant team or try to find out anything but the barest details, such as day-old rankings. Many
Web pages, such as the one shown in Figure 4-4, exist just to
keep you up-to-date.

Figure 4-4: The LinkFinder sports page.

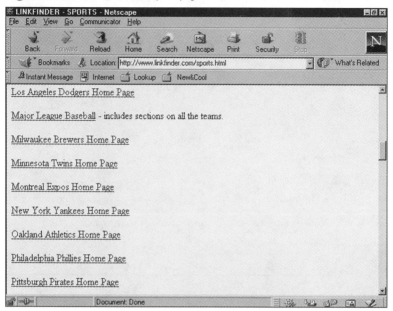

Table 4-4 gives the URLs for many of the main sports organizations:

Table 4-4: Major Sports Sites on the Web

Web site	URL
Ladies Professional Golf Association (LPGA)	www.lpga.com
Major League Baseball	www.majorleaguebaseball.com
Major League Soccer	www.mlsnet.com
NASCAR	www.nascar.com
National Basketball Association (NBA)	www.nba.com
National Football League (NFL)	www.nfl.com

Web site	URL
National Hockey League (NHL)	www.nhl.com
Professional Golfer's Association (PGA)	www.pga.com
U.S. Tennis Association (USTA)	www.usta.com

Going for the weather

Want to know whether or not it's raining in Raratonga? Snowing in Saskatchewan? Windy in Wachovia? No problem — the Web is absolutely overflowing with weather sites. You can go for the Old Farmer's Almanac Long-Range Forecast at www.almanac.com/weather/weather.html, or you can surf to the more scientific sites, such as the National Weather Service, as shown in Figure 4-5.

Figure 4-5: The National Weather Service Web site.

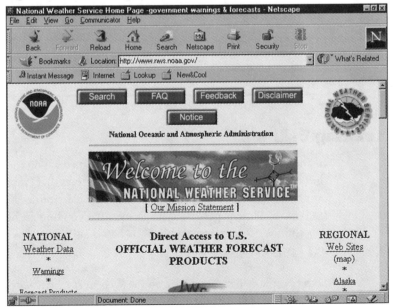

Whether you're just planning a picnic or conducting professional research, such as digging up the details of long-term hurricane patterns, you can find what you're looking for in the weather Web sites. You can view current satellite images or dig through historical images at your leisure. Some sites, wired into video cameras called *live cams,* or *Web cams,* actually enable you to look out a window thousands of miles away to see how cloudy or sunny it is. For more information, see Chapter 7.

Table 4-5 gives the URLs of several weather sites:

Table 4-5: Weather Sites on the Web

Web site	URL
AccuWeather	`www.accuweather.com/web/index.htm`
National Weather Service	`www.nws.noaa.gov`
Weather Channel	`www.weather.com/twc/homepage.twc`
Weather Underground	`www.wunderground.com/index.html`
WeatherNex	`http://cirrus.sprl.umich.edu/wxnet`
WxUSA	`www.wxusa.com`

Reading E-Zines

In addition to newspapers and the electronic media, you can find thousands and thousands of online magazines that cover every topic under the sun. Some of them are electronic versions of the same paper-based magazines that you find at the newsstands. Others are strictly Web-based and have never had a paper incarnation.

Some people call any magazine on the Web an *electronic magazine,* or *e-zine* for short (sometimes just *zine* if they really shorten it). Other people insist that electronic magazines that also appear on paper don't really qualify as e-zines but are just transcriptions of the old-style magazines. Whichever side you take in that debate, you can still find plenty of both kinds to enjoy.

E-zines cover more than the weekly or monthly news. You can find e-zines on every subject — from literature and poetry to television shows and movie idols. If you want to know about a subject, you can find an e-zine about it on the Web. Table 4-6 gives the URLs of some familiar magazines that you can read on the Web.

Table 4-6: Familiar Magazines on the Web

E-Zine	URL
Billboard	www.billboard.com
Cosmopolitan	www.cosmomag.com
Outside	www.outsidemag.com
People	www.pathfinder.com/ people/web/index.html
Popular Science	www.popsci.com
Reader's Digest	www.readersdigest.com
Utne Reader	www.utne.com

Most regular magazines that are also online have their full set of articles posted for you to read, but some magazines list only their contents, showing what's in the print issue. Among those that do post all their articles, some of them don't let you see anything but the current issue. The best ones give you full access to everything they've got, past or present.

CHAPTER 5

USING ONLINE CHAT

IN THIS CHAPTER

- Understanding chat rooms
- Picking a chat server
- Coping with IRC
- Using alternatives to IRC
- Chat room safety

You can find all kinds of online chat to jump into. To log onto chat rooms and communicate with people in them, you can use the most popular software, *Internet Relay Chat* (IRC). For a more private experience, you can also choose from among several programs for a one-on-one chat. To use the local chat facilities available on some Web sites, you can choose from among a number of proprietary chat programs, besides IRC.

This chapter tells you what chat rooms are, how to pick the right kind of chat software, what the alternatives are to the standard chat methods, and how to keep your chat room experiences safe and pleasant.

Understanding Chat Rooms

Chat rooms, or *channels* as they're called in IRC jargon, are online places where people get together to have group conversations — and just like conversations in real life, these take place live and everyone can talk all at once. To use them, you first need to fire up a chat program and log on to a chat server, which manages the chat rooms. Once on the server, you can pick the rooms in which you want to participate. Each room is devoted to a separate topic. Going into one room means that you're going to be with people talking about, say, astrology, while in another room they may be talking about politics.

The one real difference between chat rooms and real-life conversations is that chat room conversations are in print instead of by voice. You communicate with other people in the room by typing into your chat program and then sending what you typed to the chat server. Everyone in the room sees everything that anyone else in the room types.

People in chat rooms use the same kinds of emoticons and abbreviations that they use in e-mail. See Chapter 2 for more information.

Although the actual number of people in each chat room is often very small (from 1 to 100 people), a *chat network* can accommodate thousands of rooms. Consequently, you can find tens of thousands of chatters on any given network (a group of chat rooms) at any given moment. A large network typically accommodates about 40,000 to 50,000 people at a time. The more people participating, the fuller the chat rooms are.

Both in its purpose and the way it's used, IRC is a lot like CB radio. Each person on a chat server is identified by a nickname of their choosing, much as CBers are known by their "handles," and the atmosphere has the same informality and lack of structure that CBers are famous for.

Nicknames are not reserved on most IRC networks; DAL-net — one of the larger chat networks — is a rare exception because their policy allows nickname reservations (see "Choosing a Chat Server" later in this chapter). Someone else may already be using the nickname you planned to use when you logged on. Because only one person can use a particular nickname at a particular time, you want to have several nicknames ready to avoid wasting a lot of time thinking up a new one when you log on to the chat server.

You can always add a random number at the end of your usual nickname to make it unique. For example, if you call yourself "Captain" and someone else is using the same name, just call yourself "Captain1234."

Everybody in the chat room can — and often does — talk all at once. Usually, several different conversations take place simultaneously. As a result, chat room conversation is hard to follow at first. However, with a little experience, you quickly get used to it and can follow the flow without difficulty. Because each person's "talk" is preceded by their nickname, you can ignore anybody you're not listening to. So watch for the nicknames of the people that you're trying to converse with and read what they're saying.

You may want to *log* the chat — that is, save the conversation as a text file on your hard drive — if possible (not all chat programs have this capability). Doing so enables you to edit the chat later if you want or need to, eliminating every bit of input that's not a part of the conversation that you want to keep.

Picking your chat software

Basically, any chat software enables you to get online and talk. But you want to consider several factors in order to make your chats as enjoyable and easy as possible:

■ How much does the software cost? Some chat software is freeware and some is shareware.

■ Does the software let you connect to more than one chat server without having to run more than one instance of the program? (When you start the same program up more than once at a time, each one is called an *instance*.)

■ Does the software have an easy-to-use visual user interface — a simple set of icons or buttons — or do you have to memorize a bunch of arcane instructions?

■ Does the software provide a good help file that is geared to your level of expertise?

■ Does the software support the full range of IRC commands or just a limited number of them?

■ Does the software let you log a chat to a file? If so, can you simultaneously log multiple chats to separate files?

■ Does the publisher provide solid customer service support? Check for a good Web site with at least a list of Frequently Asked Questions (FAQ), such as the one shown in Figure 5-1. You should also be able to e-mail questions and perhaps even call a customer support telephone number.

Table 5-1 lists some of the most popular IRC chat software:

Table 5-1: Popular IRC Software

Chat Program	URL
Microsoft Chat	www.microsoft.com/windows/ie/chat
mIRC	www.mirc.co.uk
PIRCH	www.pirchat.com
VIRC	www.megalith.co.uk/virc
XiRCON	www.xircon.com

Some of the really sophisticated chat software, such as VIRC, go way beyond simple IRC and enable you to conduct chats via voice or even real-time video. Of course, you have to have the appropriate hardware in order to use these extra options.

Figure 5-1: The mIRC Web site's FAQ.

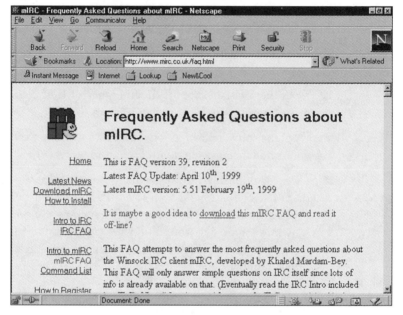

Microsoft Chat has one of the strangest interfaces of all the online chat programs. The program was originally known as "Comic Chat" because, in addition to normal text-based communication, it can create a comic book on your screen. In the panels of the comic book, the different people in the chat room appear as various odd-looking characters, and their input shows up in speech balloons within the panels. However, for this feature to work, you have to be logged on to one of the Microsoft special comic chat servers. You can still use the program on normal IRC servers by setting the program to normal text chat.

Making your own chat room

You can find chat rooms on zillions and zillions of topics. But the chance always exists that you may want to chat on a topic that's not covered or at a time when the room for that subject isn't available. Or you may want to have a private party for a variety of reasons. With your own chat room, you can do anything from having a family reunion to holding seminars.

Finally, and to some people most importantly, you're in charge in a private room. You can keep the conversation on topic, lock out uninvited and disruptive visitors, and generally make yourself at home without interruption.

This last reason is one of the keys to online chat. With a good person in charge, a chat room is a useful and enjoyable experience. If you don't like the way someone else runs a chat room, you can just make your own and run it the way you like. That way, everyone stays happy.

Choosing a Chat Server

Just as a mail server handles e-mail and a Web server processes Web pages, a chat server hosts chat rooms. However, you only have to worry about the e-mail and Web servers when you first sign up with a particular ISP and change them if you change your ISP.

For chat rooms, you may want to use a different server every time, or even several servers at one time if you find yourself getting heavily into multiple chats. If the chat room you want to go to right now isn't on the same server as the chat room you just left, you need to connect to the server where the chat room that you want is hosted.

Some chat programs let you log on to different servers with just one instance of the program running; others require you to start a different instance of the program for each server you connect to.

You can choose from among four major chat networks — Efnet, Undernet, IRCnet, and DALnet — and lots of smaller ones. And other, less stable networks come and go all the time. Although most chat programs come with a list of servers that you can simply select from, not all do. Whether or not yours does, you may wish to look at everything available to you. Table 5-2 lists the home pages for several chat networks. Each home page provides a list of some chat servers you can log onto.

Table 5-2: Major Chat Networks

Chat Network	URL
AUSTnet	www.austnet.org
ChatNet	www.chatnet.org
DALnet	www.dal.net
Efnet	www.irchelp.org/irchelp/ networks/servers/efnet.html
Galaxynet	www.galaxynet.org
IRCnet	www.irchelp.org/irchelp/ networks/servers/ircnet.html
Newnet	www.newnet.net
StarLink	www.starlink.org/starlink
Undernet	www.undernet.org

Coping with IRC

Even though it's been around for years, IRC still hasn't evolved into a truly user-friendly state. With the exception of a handful of newer programs, IRC software still expects you to memorize and manually type a bunch of arcane commands. Many of them are more like DOS-style museum pieces rather than modern software.

One of the best sources of information on IRC is the IRC Help Web site at `www.irchelp.org`.

If you're a power chat user, you may prefer the more hands-on approach. Even if you're not, some of the smaller chat programs that require the least resources on your computer system also provide the least in the way of bells and whistles. This situation is a trade-off, of course — the smaller programs that you can use on a less powerful computer often require you to do more work manually entering IRC commands. Either way, you ought to know at least the basic IRC commands. Table 5-3 shows the ones you're most likely to need:

Table 5-3: Common IRC Commands

Command	Effect
/disconnect	Shuts off your connection to the IRC server
/exit	Shuts off your connection to the IRC server and closes your IRC client
/join *channelname*	Joins the chat room specified in *channelname*
/list	Gets a list of available chat rooms
/names *channelname*	Gets a list of all the nicknames in the chat room specified in *channelname*
/nick *newname*	Changes your nickname to the one specified as *newname*
/part *channelname*	Takes you out of the chat room specified in *channelname*
/partall	Takes you out of every chat room you were connected to
/quit *message*	Functions the same way as /disconnect, except that you can specify a parting message
/say *message*	Sends *message* to the chat room
/server *address*	Connects to the chat server specified in *address*

continued

Table 5-3: *(continued)*

Command	Effect
/who *channelname*	Functions the same way as /names
/who *address*	Gets a list of all users with matching *address*

Using Alternatives to IRC

If you're not really comfortable with IRC, you can find plenty of other ways to chat online. You can carry on live, online conversations outside the usual chat rooms using several different kinds of non-IRC software. Some of the most popular programs used for this purpose are ICQ, PowWow, and AOL Instant Messenger (no, you don't have to be on AOL to use it). These programs enable you to chat either one-on-one or in chat rooms created for their users.

In addition to these programs, you can also find lots of Web-based chat rooms. To use Web-based chat rooms, you go to the Web site that hosts the chat and click the appropriate links to the chat rooms. These sites aren't run with IRC software but with proprietary programs that you get from the Web site when you log on. Depending on the site, you may find one chat room or many. If you see only one, then clicking the link takes you right to it; if you see several rooms, then you go to another page of links that lists all the chat rooms.

Chatting without IRC

Several relatively new non-IRC programs like PowWow let you connect either to an individual for a one-on-one chat session or to a group for a chat room session. In order for these programs to work, both you and the person or people you want to chat with have to be members of the same network of chat users and, of course, using the same software at the same time. You can't, for example, chat with a PowWow user by using AOL Instant Messenger. However, you can use both programs.

Table 5-4 lists the most popular non-IRC chat programs and the Web site addresses where you can find them.

Table 5-4: Popular Non-IRC Chat Programs

Program	*URL*
AOL Instant Messenger	www.newaol.com/aim
ICQ	www.mirabilis.com
PowWow	www.tribal.com

AOL Instant Messenger (AIM) comes with the Netscape Navigator Web browser and is also available for separate download. AIM is typical of this type of chat software and one of the simplest to use. From among the program's users, you establish a *buddy list,* as shown in Figure 5-2, and the software informs you when anyone on your buddy list is online. If the person's not online, you can't chat with him or her. This feature is more than a minor point of consideration. The program makes a noise to inform you when the person comes online so that you can look at your buddy list to see who it is. Other sounds indicate that a buddy has left, that someone is messaging you, and so forth. You can either accept the default sounds or supply your own. (See Chapter 7 for an explanation of sound files.)

Both ICQ and the Tribal Voice PowWow (see Figure 5-3) provide many more capabilities than AOL Instant Messenger does. For example, PowWow has built-in voice chat and Web tours (which enable you to lead a group of other Pow-Wow users to various Web sites of your choosing).

ICQ and AOL are favorites among malicious code crackers, and both programs have experienced several security violations in the past. If you use them, check frequently with their home pages to find out about fixes for any newly discovered security holes.

Figure 5-2: AOL Instant Messenger.

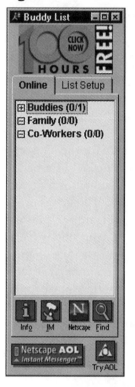

Using Web chat

You can find a number of Web-based chat rooms that use software supplied by the particular Web site. The most famous is Talk City at www.talkcity.com. (Talk City also runs a standard IRC server at chat.talkcity.com.) Figure 5-4 shows the Web page where you enter Talk City's Web-based chat rooms. Most of the other online communities (see Chapter 6) also offer Web-based chat.

Many Web-based chat programs use Java applets. So, if you've disabled Java in your Web browser, those chat programs won't work.

Figure 5-3: The PowWow home page.

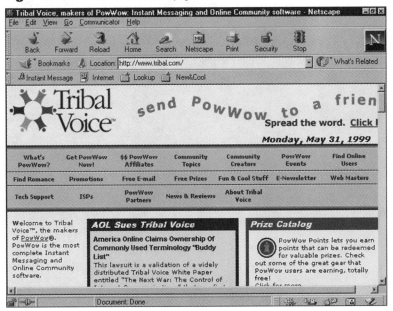

You can also find online forums on many Web sites. Forums differ from chat rooms in that they're not live. Otherwise, they're pretty similar. Forums are dedicated to a particular topic. You post messages for all the other people who use the forum, and you read any messages that the other users post. However, these messages don't go away when the chat is over. They're kept online for a long period of time so that users can read and respond to the messages at their leisure.

Whatever you post in an online forum remains there for a long time. So don't say anything you may later regret.

Figure 5-4: The Talk City chat entry.

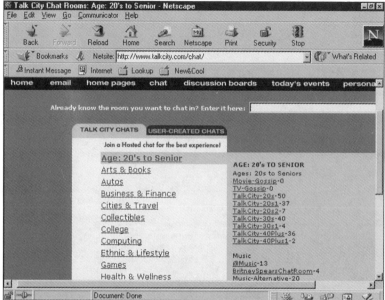

Most forums also have available some kind of search software that enables you to find messages in the forum by topic, sender, or date of posting and to follow up on all the replies that are posted to a particular message (which is called *following the thread*).

Chat Room Safety

A really important difference exists between chat rooms and the real world: You can meet practically anyone in the world online, but you're not meeting them in person. This situation means that the people you interact with may or may not be who or what you think they are.

Remaining anonymous

Many people like the fact that they can be whoever they want to be when chatting online. No official statistics exist on this, but judging from the ways people describe themselves in chat rooms, compared to the kinds of people you see in the real world, most online chatters seem to embellish their autobiographies a bit.

Such embellishment is usually harmless fiction — a couch potato may pretend that he or she is an aerobics instructor. But you need to be aware of this factor when you're in a chat room. Just accept that every man in a chat room is handsome and broad-shouldered, every woman is somehow both slender and voluptuous, and everyone has plenty of money and at least three fancy cars. This aspect calls for at least a pound or two of salt, of course.

Dealing with rude chatters

Just as people find that being rude on the telephone is easier than being rude when they're face to face with someone, the anonymity of online relationships sometimes brings out the worst in people. After all, if someone known to you only as "Spock99" gets nasty, how can you ever retaliate?

Nine times out of ten, "Spock99" turns out to be some kid with a personality problem and a modem. In many online chat rooms, a chat room host (or moderator) handles the problem and keeps the chat running smoothly.

Of course, if someone gets really out of line — for example, the person threatens you — then you should immediately report him or her to the people who run the chat server. If a host or moderator is in the chat room, he or she can use the host's authority to ban the offender from the room. In extreme cases, bans may become permanent and even extend to everyone using a particular ISP, just to make the ban stick.

You may want to keep handy the e-mail address of the chat room's security people, so that you don't have to hunt for the address when you need it.

Keeping your real life out of the chat room

You may want to keep your "real life" totally separate from your chat room life. Be careful about revealing information that would enable someone in a chat room to find you in the real world, such as where you live or work or your telephone number. Maintaining such privacy is up to you, of course, but if you do involve people you meet in chat rooms in your offline life, *be very careful.* Some people have built enduring friendships and even gotten married to people they met in chat rooms; however, you can never be sure about who you may meet there. Certainly, you never want to give out personal contact information in a public chat room, where everyone who wanders in can see it. If you do want to give someone your contact information, wait until you're in a private chat room with the person or until you know the person for at least several weeks.

Warning

Children, in particular, should be taught chat room safety. Remember that you don't really know who someone is in a chat room, including that person's age and sex. If your child wants to meet a fellow chatter in person, make sure that you go along at least the first time to ensure that the person is really who he or she claims to be. Until you see for yourself, you can't be sure that the sweet little girl your child has been talking to isn't someone else entirely.

You don't necessarily need to become paranoid about this — the Internet isn't crawling with zillions of pedophiles waiting to pounce on young victims. After all, the offline world isn't filled with car thieves, but you still lock your car doors. Just make sure you exercise the normal precautions you would take in your day-to-day, offline life.

CHAPTER 6

MEETING KINDRED SPIRITS

IN THIS CHAPTER

- Exploring online communities
- Meeting the standards
- Becoming a community guide
- Linking to Web rings

People are social animals, and this fact is every bit as true in the high-tech world of the Internet as anywhere else. People like to meet others with whom they share something in common.

Online communities were created to satisfy and serve that social need. They give people a place to belong amidst the vast wilderness of the Internet. Online communities are rapidly becoming so popular that many traditional Web portals, such as Yahoo! and Excite, are starting to look more and more like online communities every day.

In this chapter, you find out how online communities work, where to find them, and what they expect of you as a community member. You also look into becoming a community guide and take a peek at Web rings, another kind of grouping in which totally independent Web sites link to one another to create a megasite on a particular topic.

Exploring Online Communities

Online communities are super Web sites comprising members' Web sites. All online communities have something more to offer than just another Web page. Almost without exception, they offer a large line of other services to benefit you. Typically, the benefits include the following:

■ Access to online chats and forums (see Chapter 5 for more information on chat rooms and forums).

■ A free e-mail account. Some communities run regular mail servers of the POP and SMTP varieties (see Chapter 2). But many others use specialized Web-based e-mail programs that you have to use from their Web site. With a Web-based account, you can easily pick up your e-mail from any computer that has a Web browser (which is practically every computer in the world). All you have to do is browse to the appropriate Web site and punch in your user name and password to pick up your messages. That makes using Web terminals in airports and restaurants to keep track of your e-mail easy.

■ Space on their Web server for your own Web pages. The amount of Web server space varies from one community to another. But the amount is usually much more substantial than you need for any casual usage — usually about 1.9 megabytes, more than most people use for their personal home pages. Some communities give you over 10 megs to play with, which gives you plenty of room to sprawl out.

Understanding community types

Some of the most common online community varieties include the following:

■ Communities that attempt to emulate a cosmopolitan gathering. The most common theme is that of a small city. These city types, like GeoCities, are usually further broken down into smaller areas of common interest (GeoCities calls them "neighborhoods"), which may then be broken down into even more specialized parts.

■ Communities based on a particular type of work. In this type of community, you find colonies of artists, writers, musicians, and the like.

■ Communities based on a common interest other than work, such as Parent Soup, Game Land, or Seniors. Some of these types of communities — such as Children with Diabetes — exist to create a support group for people facing difficult situations.

Table 6-1 lists several online communities and the URLs of their home pages.

Table 6-1: Some Online Communities

Community	URL
Children with Diabetes	www.childrenwith diabetes.com
Game Land	www.game-land.com
GeoCities	www.geocities.com
Parent Soup	www.parentsoup.com
The Park	www.the-park.com
Seniors	www.seniors.com
Tripod	www.tripod.com
Womens.com	www.womens.com
Xoom	www.xoom.com

To join an online community, look for a link on their home page (see Figure 6-1) that contains words like "join" or "become a member" and click it. That click takes you to a form where you can fill out the necessary information to become a member.

Figure 6-1: The GeoCities main screen.

Depending on the individual community, you need to pro-vide different sorts of information. With all of them, how-ever, you have to give such information as your name, address, and phone number, as well as a current e-mail address where they can contact you. You also need to pick a user name and a password that you can use to gain access to their members-only services. Many of the communities also offer you the "opportunity" to have your personal informa-tion provided to other companies. This practice is one of the ways the communities make a profit; so if you agree to the arrangement, plan to have to deal with lots of junk mail. Of course, if the community specifies the type of material you'll receive, you may want to get on some of the mailing lists. For instance, if you're a sports fan and they ask you whether you want to receive offers on sports merchandise, you may be happy to agree.

After you complete the application, you can usually put up a Web page right away, and your e-mail account becomes active. With some communities, however, you must wait a little while before you can get into the activities. In this situation, you soon receive an e-mail message at the address that you specified in the membership form. That message contains your password.

Even if you don't have to wait, you may still receive an e-mail confirmation that contains other membership information. This information usually includes reminders about your user name and password, the URLs of help pages for the community, and the e-mail addresses of people you may need to contact for assistance.

You need to make sure that you print out your welcome message when it arrives and keep a copy of it in a file.

Paying the price

As with everything else in the world, online communities cost money — lots of money. You don't have to pay a penny to become a member of one and take advantage of all the nice things they have to offer, but someone has to pick up the check.

In addition to the communities that sell membership information, nearly all of them support themselves with online advertising. As a result, your Web page must carry whatever advertising the online community you belong to specifies. Often, that advertising takes the form of a banner at the top of your Web page. Most people who surf the Web are accustomed to banner advertising, so this arrangement isn't necessarily a reason to avoid a community.

Unfortunately, some communities are turning to more intrusive forms of advertising that are generally unacceptable on the Web, such as the use of a JavaScript popup window that overlies your Web page. These windows actually represent a second instance of a visitor's Web browser, and they're particularly annoying to visitors because the windows don't go away when the visitors leave your site. Instead, visitors have to close the windows separately. Tripod is one such community. You need to consider the annoyance factor for your users when thinking of joining such a community.

Going commercial

Online communities are commercial enterprises, despite the fact that they don't charge you to join. Consequently, they don't permit you to run your own commercial operations through them unless you pay for the privilege. Although not all online communities allow commercial Web sites, most do for a fee. Some of them even provide a great deal of assistance in getting the site up and running. GeoCities, for instance, has a section called GeoShops (`www.geocities/join/geoshops`) that includes everything you need to set up an online business.

Meeting the Standards

Online communities exercise a great deal of control over their members.

When you join an online community, you agree to certain terms and conditions that limit your ability to express yourself. Generally, these terms and conditions amount to nothing more than normal polite behavior (see Figure 6-2), although nothing limits the terms and conditions to that. How you feel about the restrictions on the language you may use and the things you may discuss is up to you. Unfortunately, how you respond is not up to you.

Figure 6-2: A typical terms agreement.

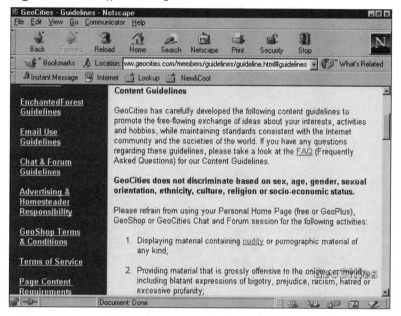

If you find the terms and conditions acceptable, you should have no problem in joining one of these communities. If you prefer not to have someone looking over your shoulder all the time, you may want to avoid the online communities.

As with everything else on the Internet, the quality and value of an online community is a result of the people who participate in it.

Becoming a Community Guide

Whether they're called hosts, guides, or something else, unpaid volunteers keep the online communities running. The number of actual paid staff is usually kept at an absolute minimum, so the volunteers do the bulk of the work.

So if you're looking for employment, this isn't a great area to focus on. The Internet has very few paid community staffers.

If you're a helping sort of person, though, and you enjoy giving newcomers a hand getting comfortable with new surroundings, then you may really enjoy serving as a community guide.

Keeping up the image

As an online guide, you must inevitably deal with people who are confused and sometimes angry. Maintaining a cheerful and positive attitude can sometimes take all you've got. You're responsible, though, for maintaining the good image of the community. Indeed, you *are* the community to the people you're dealing with.

Your duties as a guide may vary, depending on the particular features of the community you serve. You may perform technical support for people who are new to setting up Web pages. You may host an online chat. Regardless of the community you join, you can do plenty to help other members. If your community doesn't have a link that you can click to volunteer, try sending an e-mail addressed to administration@community.com (replacing community.com with the name of your community, of course), asking what you can do to help.

As a guide, you need to be well versed in your duties in order to provide the most assistance to others. For example, if you're helping people use the community's proprietary software, make sure that you know the software inside and out.

Leading chats

Leading an online chat is similar to hosting a party at your home — you want to make sure that everyone is comfortable.

Not only do you need to be conversant with the topic, you also need to be able to handle difficult situations. Try getting the shy newcomers involved in the discussion. Try using gentle humor with anyone who's hostile or as a way to deflect difficult situations.

Sometimes, someone in the chat room persists in being disruptive no matter what you say or do. Depending upon the particular community, you may or may not have the authority to deal with disruption directly. If not, contact someone in authority at the community, who can come in and solve the problem.

Linking to Web Rings

If online communities aren't your cup of tea, but you still want to associate yourself with others who share a common interest, you may want to consider joining a Web ring. *Web rings* are groups of separate Web sites on a similar topic. Although each Web site is completely independent of all the others in the ring, they support each other and provide a nice way for people to find lots of information on the ring's topic.

Every Web site in the ring offers a special link section somewhere. Usually, this link section is at or near the bottom of the Web site's home page and contains links to the ring's home page as well as to the previous and next sites in the ring. Some link sections also provide a random link that takes you somewhere else in the Web ring each time you click it.

As you browse the Web, look for links on the pages you find. They often lead you to lots of other places that you will want to see.

Web rings exist for nearly every topic in the universe. You can find Web rings intended for computer graphics artists, jewelers, UFO enthusiasts, music lovers, medieval and

Renaissance re-enactors — you name it. Many Web rings are based in the WebRing Directory at www.webring.org, which is a good place to start if you want to locate an existing Web ring or start one of your own. You can't beat the price; the service is free.

CHAPTER 7

USING INTERNET AUDIO AND VIDEO

IN THIS CHAPTER

- Understanding file types
- Using plug-ins
- Getting radio and TV on the Net
- Exploring music and movie sites

Internet audio and video are just about the most exciting advances in Net technology to come along since the invention of the modem. For years, the only sound you could get was an error buzz if something went wrong, or the occasional beep or ping.

But sound and video take up a lot of space compared to simple things like e-mail messages. And the technology to handle such large files over the Internet was developed only fairly recently.

Now, you can use your computer to check out video clips from the latest movies or sound samples from a new album, or even to watch television shows that are rebroadcast over the Web. Some new television stations exist only on the World Wide Web and have no outside broadcast presence. This chapter tells you what you need to know about sound and video files, the types of software you need to see and hear them, and how to get radio, TV, and movie clips.

Understanding File Types

Sound and video files come in various types. Just as, when dealing with static graphics files, you have GIF, JPEG, and others, several file types convey these other types of information. Any type of audio or video link that you click from a site on the Web causes one of these files to be downloaded.

Audio files

Currently, the hot file type for audio is MP3. But you may also run into AU, RA, WAV, MIDI, AIFF, and a host of others. The older varieties, such as WAV files, require you to download the entire file before you can hear anything. Newer formats such as RealAudio (see Figure 7-1) offer *streaming audio,* which means that the file starts playing right away when you click its link and you can listen at the same time the file downloads to your system.

Figure 7-1:   The Real home page.

Video files

Common video file formats include AVI, MOV, MPG (or MPEG), and FLI. As with audio files, streaming video is rapidly becoming so popular on the Web that the older file formats — such as AVI and MOV — will undoubtedly end up in a computing museum in the near future.

Using Plug-Ins

In order for Web site links to video and audio files to work, you need to have the appropriate software on your computer. Because Web browsers come with only a limited ability to play sound and video, programs called *plug-ins* are often required. Plug-ins give your Web browser additional features beyond what it originally came with.

Needing plug-ins

Generally, you don't have to concern yourself with having the right plug-in ahead of time. If you run across a Web site link that goes to a file requiring a plug-in, you get a popup dialog box that notifies you. That dialog box either gives you the option of downloading and installing the plug-in right away or, at least, gives you a link to the home page of the company that makes the plug-in, so you can do it manually.

You have to shut down your Web browser and fire it up again in order for a newly installed plug-in to work, because plug-ins are loaded at startup.

If you want to be fully prepared, you can go ahead and load every plug-in on the planet, but that's really going a bit overboard. The more plug-ins you have, the slower your Web browser starts because they all need to load at startup. However, the plug-ins don't affect anything once you're browsing.

You should probably have, at a minimum, the following plug-ins:

- Beatnik, a popular music playing plug-in.

- Crescendo, similar to Beatnik, but from another software publisher.

- QuickTime, the movie player originally for the Macintosh.

- RealAudio (which includes RealVideo capabilities), which is commonly found on news sites, among others.

These, together with your Web browser's native sound and video capabilities, cover most of what you run across. You can get any other plug-ins if you need them.

Getting plug-ins

The best source on the Web for information on plug-ins and links to their home pages is the Netscape Plug-Ins page at `http://home.netscape.com/plugins/` (see Figure 7-2). Microsoft does not have a similar page, although you can get plug-ins for Internet Explorer via their page at `www.microsoft.com/ie/download/` — just select Add-ons.

If you want to see what plug-ins you currently have, you can select Help⇨About Plug-Ins from the menu in Netscape Navigator. Unfortunately, Internet Explorer doesn't have this feature. Instead, Internet Explorer plug-ins are registered as ActiveX controls.

Not all plug-ins work on all computers. Check to see if the plug-in you want works on your system by reading the details on its Web page before you download it.

Figure 7-2:   The Netscape Plug-Ins page.

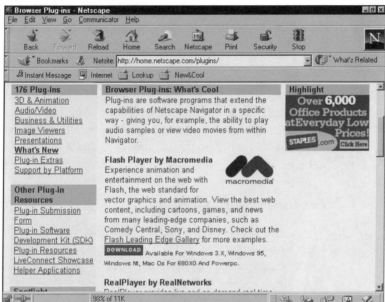

Getting Radio and TV on the Net

Lots of radio and television stations have their own sites on the World Wide Web. Many have gone that extra and obvious step to include audio and video of their shows that you can get right in your Web browser.

Finding traditional stations

Some channels, like ZDTV (www.zdtv.com), can be found on both cable and the Web. The same is true of many stations. Normal stations that you find on cable, satellite, and broadcast all have their own unique identifiers already assigned (television or radio). So all you usually have to do to find a particular station's Web site is to type in their call letters. If you're looking for WABC, then type in **www.wabc.com**. If you're looking for CNN, type in **www.cnn.com**. Odds are pretty good that you can zero right in on the desired site.

You can usually listen to sports games live without having to know the station. You only have to go to the team's home page. They normally have a link for any radio or TV broadcast that you can get on the Web.

If that technique doesn't work — and it usually is the fastest way — you can drop in to the Web site at TVFind (www.tvfind.com) to locate the station. At TVFind, you can search by state, call letter, or channel number, and the results include a link to the station's Web site, if the station has one.

Exploring Web stations

The cost of broadcasting on the World Wide Web is much lower than starting up a television network. As you can guess, a lot of people are taking a serious look at the Web as a means of sending TV shows to viewers. And some have started strictly Web-oriented broadcast networks.

Of course, the quality of shows done as Webcasts is pretty low compared to telecasts. The practical result is that the TV shows that you get on the Web are just a few inches across. For a society used to ever larger and larger television screens, this situation is a major step downward.

Nonetheless, such stations exist, and it's only a matter of time until the technology is developed that allows full-screen Webcasts. Meanwhile, you may want to check out Pseudo (www.pseudo.com) and TV on the Web (www.tvontheweb.com) for an early look at the future of television.

Exploring Music and Movie Sites

Tons of Internet music and movie Web sites exist, and more are added every day. If a new album or film is coming out, odds are pretty good that it's going to have a Web presence.

Finding movie sites

The World Wide Web's visual interface is the perfect place to showcase movies, and the movie industry has been quick to cater to the desires of the Web browsing public.

Movie promotion now normally includes a Web site with short video clips from the film, along with still photos and perhaps a few cuts from the soundtrack.

Tip

If a new movie is out, try typing in the name of the movie in the address box of your Web browser. If the name of the movie is "moviexyz," type in **www.moviexyz.com** and let your browser do the rest. If the studio's marketing department has come close to doing their job, you're very likely to land right on their new movie Web site.

Table 7-1 lists the URLs of some of the major movie studios:

Table 7-1: Some Major Movie Studios Online

Movie Studio	URL
20th Century Fox	`www.foxmovies.com`
Disney Studios	`http://disney.go.com/StudioOperations`
Paramount Pictures	`www.paramount.com/motion picture/homemp.html`
Sony Pictures	`www.spe.sony.com/movies`
Universal Studios	`www.universalstudios.com/universal_pictures`
Warner Brothers	`www.movies.warnerbros.com`

If you can't find what you want through any of these sites, try searching through the Web sites of MovieClicks.com at `www.movieclicks.com` or Movies.Net at `www.movies.net`.

Finding music sites

Record companies aren't slouches when it comes to using the Internet to promote their new releases, either. Sometimes, the Web is the first chance you have to hear new music.

Table 7-2 lists some of the major record companies and the URLs where you can find info on their artists:

Table 7-2: Major Record Labels on the Web

Record Company	URL
Atlantic Records	www.atlantic-records.com
CMC International Records	www.rockuniverse.com/index_cmc.html
Epic Records	www.epicrecords.com/EpicCenter/docs/index.qry
Fuel 2000	www.fuel2000.com
Reprise Records	www.RepriseRec.com
Warner Bros. Records	www.wbr.com
Windham Hill	www.windham.com

If you don't have any luck with the major music recording companies, you can use the Argus Music Searcher at www.fuzzlogic.com/argus/ to find nearly everything you want about music resources on the Web. Just punch in the name of the artist or the title of the song. Then you can click any button on the form to hunt down Web sites dealing with the artist, CD stores that sell the artist's music, or just about anything else you want to know.

CHAPTER 8

AVOIDING COMMON PROBLEMS

IN THIS CHAPTER

- Avoiding viruses
- Keeping transactions secure
- Coping with urban legends
- Troubleshooting for the Internet

As you work and play on the Internet, common things that happen to Netizens will probably happen to you. This chapter gets you wise ahead of time and helps you get past some problems before they come along.

Avoiding Viruses

Viruses are the great bugaboo of the Internet. *Viruses* are programs capable of replicating themselves that can do damage to your computer. Viruses aren't mutants — most were created by someone with a great deal of computer knowledge. An unfortunate reality is that some people carefully study computer science, but pervert their knowledge to harm other people, even total strangers against whom they could not possibly harbor any legitimate ill will.

Viruses are quite common. Thousands are floating around the Internet. While most viruses do little or no significant damage, even if your system does become infected, other viruses can have a devastating impact. Fortunately, with modern virus-checking software, dealing with a computer virus is considerably easier than dealing with just about any other problem you have in life.

Understanding viruses

Remember that viruses are programs. This fact is important because not all computer files are programs. For example, an image file isn't a program, nor is an e-mail message. In order to infect your system, a virus has to be run. A virus can't infect a computer simply by being downloaded.

Unfortunately, telling what is and isn't a program isn't as simple as it used to be. Microsoft Word files, for example, used to be just a fancy type of text file. However, today Word files — or any other Microsoft Office file — can contain *macros*, which are a type of program. As a result, viruses can be spread in word processing files, spreadsheet files, and so forth.

Tip

In practical terms, this means that you should never use any program whose source you aren't familiar with, unless you first run an antivirus program to check it. While you're usually safe with any program you get from a reliable source, you can't ever be totally certain. Some viruses have even occasionally shown up in commercial software packages.

Because of this situation, you have to watch out for attachments in your e-mail. The e-mail message itself is not a problem (despite constant rumors to the contrary). But programs can be sent along with an e-mail message. If you get an attachment and you don't know what it is, your best and safest course of action is to delete it without even thinking twice.

Some newer viruses spread themselves by using your own computer's address book. When they're run, they read all the e-mail addresses in it and then send copies of themselves to your friends and associates in e-mail messages that come from you. This is one very good reason why you should never trust an attachment unless you were expecting it (and you should be cautious even then).

Getting antivirus software

Lots of antivirus programs are available. You can buy them in the store or download them from the Internet. Two of the most popular are Norton AntiVirus and McAfee VirusScan, but any major brand can save your bacon if you're infected. Make sure that you have an antivirus program on your system and use it.

Table 8-1 lists the URLs of the top companies that sell antivirus software.

Table 8-1: Antivirus Software Sources

Program	URL
Dr. Solomon's	`www.drsolomon.com/home/home.cfm`
Integrity Master	`www.stiller.com/intmast.htm`
McAfee VirusScan	`www.mcafee.com`
Norton AntiVirus	`www.symantec.com/nav/index_product.html`

In addition to selling you the programs, these companies provide up-to-date virus information and debunk rumors. They're very good at both because they make their living by keeping track of these things. Figure 8-1 shows the virus information page at Symantec, makers of Norton AntiVirus.

Warning

Make sure that you regularly update your antivirus software so it can recognize and deal with the latest viruses. All major antivirus companies provide online updating capabilities.

Figure 8-1: Symantec virus information page.

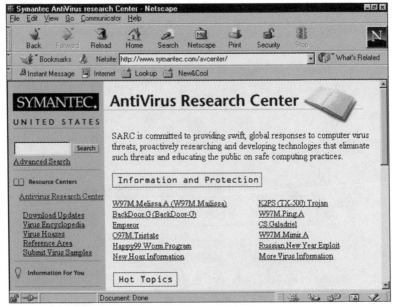

Keeping Transactions Secure

Contrary to many scare stories in the media, the Internet is not a dangerous place to use your credit cards. At least, the Internet is no more dangerous than a trip to the mall. Face it, when you hand your credit card to someone in a store, you probably know nothing about that person. For all you know, that person may be keeping copies of every charge that comes his or her way. Credit card fraud existed long before online shopping arrived.

In fact, when ordering online, you find that security is much tougher than you're used to dealing with in stores. Using secure Web servers, you can be certain that nobody but you and the company you're ordering from can get any information about the transaction.

Most companies that take orders online make a big deal about the fact that they use secure servers, so finding out which ones have them is not hard. And just to make sure, your Web browser tells you that you're on a secure Web page when you're placing the order:

- With Netscape Navigator, you see a little padlock icon in the bottom-left corner of the screen. When you're not at a secure site, the padlock is open; when you are at a secure page, the padlock is closed (see Figure 8-2).

Figure 8-2:   Navigator at a secure site.

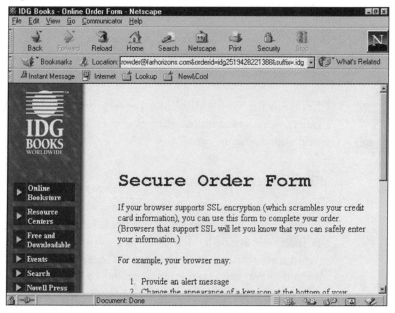

- With Internet Explorer, you see the padlock icon only if you're at a secure site (it's more in the middle at the bottom).

When you know you're at a secure Web page, you can fill out the form with confidence that your order is being processed in complete confidentiality.

Coping with Urban Legends

One of the characteristics of the Internet is that it's the fastest way to spread information ever invented. Of course, that means that the Internet is also the fastest way to spread misinformation as well. When a rumor flies over the Net, it really flies.

The hallmark of nearly every rumormonger on the Net is that the person asks you to PLEASE SEND THIS TO EVERY-ONE YOU KNOW — usually just like that, in all caps. Instead of cluttering up the Net with junk mail, ask yourself, "Do I know the person who originated this?" If the answer is no, then just delete it.

If you're on the Net for even a few weeks, you're bound to find at least one of these in your mailbox. We cover just a few of the more common ones. Don't say we didn't warn ya!

Check out the Guide to Urban Legends and Folklore at `http://urbanlegends.about.com` for the latest information about urban legends.

Virus warning hoaxes

Most virus warnings that fly around in e-mail are hoaxes. Creating panic about viruses is easy because most folks on the Internet have little idea how viruses work. These fake warnings are usually very easy to spot. The usual virus hoax claims that you can infect your computer by the simple act of reading an e-mail message, which is not true. Furthermore, they often claim that the virus alert came from Microsoft. Microsoft is a software publishing company; they don't issue virus alerts. But Microsoft is a name that most people recognize, so the hoaxsters often throw it in for effect. If you have any concern about a virus, check out the legitimate virus warnings listed on the antivirus software sites in Table 8-1, earlier in this chapter.

Tearjerker hoaxes

If you get any messages about poor, helpless children who are at death's door, and just want to hear from you before they die, it's a golden opportunity to hit your Delete key.

Nasty company hoaxes

The Mrs. Fields/Nieman Marcus cookie hoax is still floating around, a classic example of the kind of garbage that hoaxsters love to push. In this story, someone asks for the cookie recipe, the people at the store say, "Sure. We'll mail it to you." When the recipe arrives, it comes with a bill for hundreds or thousands of dollars. Right. Uh, folks, ask yourself this: If you made a living with a particular recipe, would you let anyone else look at it for any amount of money?

Bad food hoaxes

According to an awful lot of e-mail messages from people that you never heard of, all sorts of incredibly gross things are being found in the food at popular restaurants, especially fast-food joints. Somehow, the mainstream media always fails to report these astonishing cases.

Write your senator hoaxes

A tremendous amount of legislation never happened except in the minds of e-mail hoaxsters — the modem tax, the post office tax on e-mail messages, and so forth. Most of these are designed to panic Netizens into action with threats to annihilate the Internet. Very few politicians would willingly throw their careers away by angering such a loud and well-to-do political force as the Netizens. Don't pass this kind of thing on unless you first check with your congressperson.

Chain letter hoaxes

If you get an e-mail message that promises you untold riches, free vacations to Bermuda and Tahiti, or anything else that you don't expect to get in the course of a normal day, you can pretty well bet that the message is a hoax. If the message claims that you can get all these wonderful things merely by sending a copy of the message to lots of other people, you've got a definite piece of garbage on your hands. And, if the message mentions the *Guinness Book of World Records,* regardless of what else it says, it's a sure-fire hoax.

Troubleshooting for the Internet

In anything as complex as the Internet, things are bound to go wrong. The astonishing fact — and a great tribute to the engineers who built the Internet — is that so few things do.

Here are a few of the more common problems that you're likely to face and some simple solutions for them.

Breaking out of frames

When you're surfing the Web and you go to a page that has frames, you often find yourself stuck within those frames when you go to another page. The frame stays with you no matter where you go. Getting around this problem is fairly easy with either of the major Web browsers.

In Netscape Navigator, follow these steps:

1. Right-click within the frame.

2. From the popup menu, select Open Frame in New Window.

3. When the page opens up in a new window (meaning in a new instance of Navigator), close down the first version.

In Internet Explorer, you have to do a bit more monkeying. Follow these steps:

1. Hit your Back button to return to the page you came from.

2. Right click the link you followed.

3. From the popup menu, select Open in New Window.

4. When the page opens up in a new window, close down the first version.

Failing to connect to a Web server

Getting a Server Not Found error is a common occurrence and often means that you can't get through. Usually, the Web server you're trying to reach is down, either temporarily or permanently. But often this message just indicates a glitch in the Net that keeps you from getting through, so try twice before you give up. We've gotten through thousands of times by just trying again after getting an error message.

Handling returned e-mail messages

Sometimes, the e-mail message that you send is returned to you undelivered. The error message reporting this may tell you that the address doesn't exist. If you don't think the message is right, try again. Waiting a few hours before resending the message is best. That's usually enough time for the network administrator at the receiving end to find and solve the problem.

CLIFFSNOTES REVIEW

Use this CliffsNotes Review to practice what you've learned in this book and to build your confidence in doing the job right the first time. After you work through the review questions, the scenario questions, the visual test, and the fun and useful practice projects, you're well on your way to achieving your goal of surfing the Internet like a pro.

Q&A

1. IRC stands for

   a. Internet Ready Chat

   b. Internal Relay Card

   c. Internet Relay Chat

2. Viruses can be found in

   a. Image files

   b. Programs

   c. E-mail messages

3. To complain about unsolicited commercial e-mail, you

   a. Send a nasty response to the sender.

   b. Notify the postmaster at your ISP.

   c. Call the FBI.

4. If your user name is kyle and your ISP is aeiouandy.com, what is your e-mail address?

   a. kyle@aeiouandy.com

   b. aeiouandy.com.kyle

   c. kyle.aeiouandy@com

5. What does the Back button in your Web browser do?

   a. Takes you back to your home page

   b. Takes you to the last Web page you visited

   c. Reloads the current Web page

6. Why is it a good idea to hook up a phone to your modem?

_____

7. What are the three Boolean search operators?

_____

Answers: (1) c. (2) b. (3) b. (4) a. (5) b. (6) So you can check to see if the phone line works. (7) AND, OR, and NOT.

Scenarios

1. You receive a file attachment along with an e-mail message. You don't know what it is, and you don't know the person who sent it. You should _____.

2. You hear on the news that a new virus has been found and it's set to go off in a week. Even though you already have antivirus software, you should still _____.

3. You find a Web site you want to return to later. You should _____.

4. You download a file that ends in .zip. In order to make it useable, you need to _____.

Answers: (1) Delete the attachment. (2) Download the latest update from the software publisher and run the antivirus program again. (3) Bookmark the site. (4) Use an unzipping program like PKZIP.

Visual Test

In the Internet Explorer Web browser's Internet Options dialog box, the Use Default button does what?

a. Sets the page you're at to be your home page.

b. Sets the Microsoft home page as your home page.

c. Sets the page listed in the Address box as your home page.

Answer: b.

Consider This

- Did you know that you can visit an IRC channel called #Newbies where you can ask questions? Drop in and get some expert help from folks who are glad to lend a hand.

- Did you know that you can have more than one of each kind of program? Feel free to test several e-mail, chat, or Web programs all at once. You can even use two chat programs at once to talk to yourself.

Practice Projects

1. Visit several online communities. Set up free e-mail accounts and Web pages on them. See Chapter 6 for more information.

2. Find an IRC server and join a chat room on it. See Chapter 5 for more information.

3. Find a Web site that you like and set it to be your home page. See Chapter 3 for more information.

CLIFFSNOTES RESOURCE CENTER

The learning doesn't need to stop here. CliffsNotes Resource Center shows you the best of the best — links to the best information in print and online about the Internet. Look for all the terrific resources at your favorite bookstore or local library and on the Internet. When you're online, make your first stop www.cliffsnotes.com, where you can find more incredibly useful information about the Internet.

Books

This CliffsNotes book is one of many great books about the Internet published by IDG Books Worldwide, Inc. So if you want some great next-step books, check out some of these other publications:

Dummies 101: Creating Web Pages, by Kim Komando, takes you a step further than surfing the Web. Why not create your own Web page? Learn about using HTML and adding graphic images, sound, and animation to a Web page. IDG Books Worldwide, Inc. $24.99.

Dummies 101: The Internet for Windows 98, by Hy Bender and Margaret Levine Young, shows you how to use the Internet. Now that your PC is set up and ready to go online, you need to find out about surfing the Web for people, places, and other information. You find out about sending and receiving e-mail and discussion groups online. IDG Books Worldwide, Inc. $24.99.

Teach Yourself the Internet, by David A. Crowder and Rhonda Crowder, gives you detailed step-by-step instructions for browsing the World Wide Web, customizing your Web browser, sending e-mail, creating your own Web pages, and much, much more. IDG Books Worldwide, $19.99.

You can easily find books published by IDG Books Worldwide, Inc., in your favorite bookstores, at the library, on the Internet, and at a store near you. We also have three Web sites that you can use to read about all the books we publish:

`www.cliffsnotes.com`

`www.dummies.com`

`www.idgbooks.com`

Internet

Check out these Web sites for more information about the Internet:

All About the Internet, `http://shell.rmi.net/~kgr/internet/`, takes you to where you can find current and past articles to help you fill in your knowledge.

Folks Online, `www.folksonline.com`, is where you can explore chat rooms and message boards for Internet beginners and maybe even find some e-mail pals.

ISP Finder, `www.ispfinder.com`, is a service that lists thousands of Internet service providers.

ISP Locator, `http://boardwatch.internet.com/isp/locateisp.html`, takes you to *Boardwatch* magazine's ISP Locator. Just find your state and click the appropriate area code to get a listing of ISPs in your area.

Matisse's Glossary of Internet Terms, `www.matisse.net/files/glossary.html`, is a marvelous resource where you can find the plain meaning of that confusing jargon you run across from time to time.

NetWelcome, www.netwelcome.com, leads to the award-winning NetWelcome site for newbies, where you can find simple descriptions of the first things you need to know and links to all sorts of fun and useful resources for you to explore.

Newbie dot Org, www.newbie.org, has different levels for beginning, intermediate, and advanced Net users, so you can grow along with it.

NewbieNET, www.newbie.net, takes you to NewbieNET, where you can take the Cyber Course or explore the Newbie Home Pages.

Newbies Anonymous: A Newcomer's Guide to the Internet, www.geocities.com/TheTropics/1945/index1.htm, is where you find Driver's Ed for the Internet and the Weird, Unusual, Freaky, and Fun (WUFF) links pages.

Ozline, www.ozline.com/learning/stumble.html, is the wonderful Surf, Stumble, Search, and Lurch Web site. Here, you find information on search engines, links for educators, and some very unusual but fun links to boot.

Rob's Short Tutorial and Links for Newbies, www.mindspring.com/~icarus1/newbies.html, leads to the home of Rob's 15 Minute Internet Tutorial.

Terry's Netiquette Page, www.voicenet.com/~terryr/netqtt.html, is where you learn the do's and don'ts that let you get along with other people on the Internet. Terry performs a great service for the Net — be sure to check out the link at the bottom of the page to the Netiquette Web Ring that Terry runs.

WebNovice, www.webnovice.com, is where you can find a newbies' forum, tutorials, tips, and tricks.

Next time you're on the Internet, don't forget to drop by www.cliffsnotes.com. We created an online Resource Center that you can use today, tomorrow, and beyond.

Send Us Your Favorite Tips

In your quest for knowledge, have you ever experienced that sublime moment when you figure out a trick that saves time or trouble? Perhaps you realized you were taking ten steps to accomplish something that could take two. Or you found a little-known workaround that achieved great results. If you've discovered a useful tip that helped you browse the Internet more effectively, and you'd like to share it, the CliffsNotes staff would love to hear from you. Go to our Web site at www.cliffsnotes.com and look for the Talk to Us button. If we select your tip, we may publish it as part of *CliffsNotes Daily,* our exciting, free e-mail newsletter. To find out more, or to subscribe to the newsletter, go to www.cliffsnotes.com on the Web.

INDEX

continued

Z

COMING SOON FROM CLIFFSNOTES

Online Shopping

HTML

Choosing a PC

Beginning Programming

Careers

Windows 98 Home Networking

eBay Online Auctions

PC Upgrade and Repair

Business

Microsoft Word 2000

Microsoft PowerPoint 2000

Finance

Microsoft Outlook 2000

Digital Photography

Palm Computing

Investing

Windows 2000

Online Research

IDG
BOOKS
WORLDWIDE

COMING SOON FROM CLIFFSNOTES
Buying and Selling on eBay

Have you ever experienced the thrill of finding an incredible bargain at a specialty store or been amazed at what people are willing to pay for things that you might toss in the garbage? If so, then you'll want to learn about eBay — the hottest auction site on the Internet. And CliffsNotes *Buying and Selling on eBay* is the shortest distance to eBay proficiency. You'll learn how to:

- Find what you're looking for, from antique toys to classic cars

- Watch the auctions strategically and place bids at the right time

- Sell items online at the eBay site

- Make the items you sell attractive to prospective bidders

- Protect yourself from fraud

Here's an example of how the step-by-step CliffsNotes learning process simplifies placing a bid at eBay:

1. Scroll to the Web page form that is located at the bottom of the page on which the auction item itself is presented.

2. Enter your registered eBay username and password and enter the amount you want to bid. A Web page appears that lets you review your bid before you actually submit it to eBay. After you're satisfied with your bid, click the Place Bid button.

3. Click the Back button on your browser until you return to the auction listing page. Then choose View⇨Reload (Netscape Navigator) or View⇨Refresh (Microsoft Internet Explorer) to reload the Web page information. Your new high bid appears on the Web page, and your name appears as the high bidder.